DRIVING FEAR OUT OF THE WORKPLACE

D·R·I·V·I·N·G
FEAR
OUT·OF·THE
WORKPLACE

HOW TO OVERCOME
THE INVISIBLE BARRIERS
TO QUALITY,
PRODUCTIVITY,
AND INNOVATION

Kathleen D. Ryan
Daniel K. Oestreich

Jossey-Bass Publishers
San Francisco • Oxford • 1991

DRIVING FEAR OUT OF THE WORKPLACE
How to Overcome the Invisible Barriers to
Quality, Productivity, and Innovation
by Kathleen D. Ryan and Daniel K. Oestreich

Copyright © 1991 by: Jossey-Bass Inc., Publishers
350 Sansome Street
San Francisco, California 94104
&
Jossey-Bass Limited
Headington Hill Hall
Oxford OX3 0BW

Library of Congress Cataloging-in-Publication Data

Ryan, Kathleen, date.
 Driving fear out of the workplace : how to overcome the invisible
barriers to quality, productivity, and innovation / Kathleen D.
Ryan, Daniel K. Oestreich. — 1st ed.
  p.   cm. — (The Jossey-Bass management series)
 Includes bibliographical references and index.
 ISBN 1-55542-317-5 (alk. paper)
  1. Organizational effectiveness.   2. Work environment.   3. Fear.
I. Oestreich, Daniel K., date.   II. Title.   III. Series.
HD58.9.R93   1991
658.5—dc20   90-47648
                                                        CIP

Manufactured in the United States of America

The paper in this book meets the guidelines for
permanence and durability of the Committee on
Production Guidelines for Book Longevity of the
Council on Library Resources.

A BARD PRODUCTIONS BOOK

Copy Editing: Helen Hyams
Text Design: Suzanne Pustejovsky
Jacket Design: Suzanne Pustejovsky
Composition/Production: Round Rock Graphics

FIRST EDITION
 HB Printing   10 9 8 7 6 5 4 3 2
Code 9115

The Jossey-Bass
Management Series

CONTENTS

■

PART ONE: THE DYNAMICS OF FEAR

PART TWO: HOW FEAR OPERATES IN ORGANIZATIONS

ix

PART FOUR:
CONCLUSION: CREATING A QUALITY ORGANIZATION

PREFACE

■

Attempting to succeed amid the business realities of the 1990s, executives and managers are discovering many barriers. These go beyond the familiar challenges of global competition, shrinking resources, and the continued urgency to produce short-term profits while ensuring long-term success. The emerging dilemmas include the significant gap between work-force skills and business needs, the appropriate use of new technologies, and the difficulty of institutionalizing progressive methods for managing people. Hidden behind these barriers one may also recognize the presence of fear. We see fear as a background phenomenon that undermines the commitment, motivation, and confidence of people at work. It is most easily observed as a reluctance to speak up about needed changes, improvements, or other important work issues. To move forward into this new decade, organizations must break through this barrier to create environments where quality, productivity, and innovation can flourish.

The problem, as a vice-president of a Fortune 500 company told us, is that fear is at the root of "all the time people spend in meetings not saying what's really on their minds." These silences, built into organizations at all levels, plague most managers. They represent the absence of ideas or enthusiasm, suggestions that never go beyond the ordinary, conversations that circle the problem but never pin it down, unfinished business that leads to poor follow-through and mediocre results. At the hectic pace managers are expected to sustain, it is hard to understand and easy to ignore the moments when fear intervenes. To help create a better environment, this book describes:

- The areas people cannot talk about openly at work
- The reasons they do not speak up
- The impact fear has on individuals and organizations

- Practical methods managers can use to encourage people to speak openly and turn patterns of fear into creativity and trust

Why We Have Written This Book

Our work on this topic has been inspired primarily by our consulting experiences over the last several years. We have worked in very different organizational settings: one as an independent external consultant with a variety of ongoing clients, and the other as a full-time training and organization development consultant for a mid-sized city. We both have observed the reluctance of talented managers who worked for good bosses to speak up about organizational issues and needed improvements. When we would inquire about people's hesitation, we both heard lines such as:

    66 *You've got to be careful on that subject.* 99

    66 *You can never be fully honest around here.* 99

    66 *You just never know how [boss's name] will react.* 99

We found that these experiences corresponded with the teachings of W. Edwards Deming and others involved with continuous quality improvement. Deming asserts in his fourteen obligations of management that quality is impossible where people are afraid to tell the truth. Scrap and breakage get hidden, numbers and schedules are misrepresented, and bad products are forwarded to customers because the quality assurance inspector knows better than to stop the line. Deming admonishes managers to drive out fear so that everyone can participate meaningfully in the organization.

We pursued this topic and sought out work done by others that could help us understand the causes and impact of fear in organizations, and solutions to this problem. We did not find any major work that directly targeted what we wanted to know. Several fine books and articles were helpful to us and many of them are referenced in the coming pages, but their focus—while important and thought-provoking—was usually peripheral to the issue of fear in the workplace. We saw a gap and decided to do our part to fill it.

Our Audience

Throughout this book we refer to our readers by the general term *manager*. By this we mean anyone who has some type of supervisory capacity—from executives through first-line supervisors. We assume that most of our readers therefore will wear two hats at once: boss and employee. Whenever we can, we encourage people to apply what they learn while wearing one hat to what they need to do while wearing the other one.

Beyond those with management responsibility, we think *Driving Fear Out of the Workplace* will also be helpful to human resources and quality management consultants. As the experts on people and quality, these individuals are naturally sensitive to the presence and negative impact of fear.

Regardless of their position, we picture our readers as having a spirit that is committed to organizational improvement. They are women and men who know that things have to change and want to play a role in this transformation. They are individuals who understand the current implications in the old saying: "If you always do what you have always done, you will always get what you have always got." They already know or suspect that fear is an impediment, and they are willing to address the challenges, recognizing full well that improvements may require some aspect of personal growth and development.

What to Expect from This Book

Our exploration of fear is based on interviews with 260 people in twenty-two organizations around the United States, as well as on our consulting background. We asked people about experiences with fear at work in confidential one-on-one interviews and small-group discussions. Thus we can bring our concepts to life through many stories and vignettes. While the details are modified—we could not have obtained this sensitive information without guaranteeing anonymity—each story we tell is real.

In addition to providing a broader understanding of the issues through our stories and analysis of fear, we make extensive suggestions for overturning the patterns of fear. We have provided a wide range of options and potential strategies that can be customized for many types of work environments. Overall, we have aimed for the following types of reactions from our readers:

    66 *So that's what's going on! I never realized it!* **99**

    66 *Given the way recent events have gone, I can see where my employees might feel that way.* **99**

    66 *Here's something worth talking about with my group.* **99**

    66 *I bet this strategy would work for us.* **99**

Many of the stories we tell are about managers who unconsciously do things that cause their employees to be afraid. We offer descriptions of these negative behaviors as helpful examples of what *not* to do. We hope our readers will appreciate this method and our intention—which has nothing to do with manager bashing. We know from our experiences the great dedication and commitment the vast majority of managers make to their jobs, and we respect the many very difficult aspects of their roles.

Fear Is Not an Easy Topic to Explore

In the last two and a half years, we have learned much about fear and the workplace dynamics surrounding it. We have also learned a great deal about ourselves, our communication patterns, our attitudes about collaboration, and our values. Some of this has not been easy. We expect that as you read through the chapters that follow, you may have similar experiences. There are two challenges that readers may face:

1. To examine the patterns of fear, one must look at the less optimistic side of organizations. It is not pleasant to read or think about some of the illustrations in which people, quality, and productivity have been damaged by fear. But looking at this information is vitally important because it holds the key to turning around negativity in an organization. This is not an easy task; it requires some below-the-surface reflection and learning. We counsel patience and careful study of this material, knowing that it leads to positive, realistic strategies for developing trust.

2. To turn around the patterns of fear one must be willing to take risks which may threaten one's image or sense of personal credibility. Many of the action steps we recommend require higher levels of involvement and risk taking than suggestions found in other types of management books. Every attempt one makes to improve an organization by reducing fear presents the opportunity to learn something new about oneself and one's relationships with others. This is not always a comfortable experience because it can test personal assumptions, beliefs, and communication patterns. However, we see this as an entirely "doable" challenge. It is particularly important for managers whose desire for personal and professional improvement is inextricably linked to the possibilities for improvement in their organizations.

In spite of the challenges, there are many rewards for reflecting on fear and taking action to reduce it. With reduced levels of fear and increased levels of trust, people are more committed to their work and to their organizations. They are enthusiastic about what they do and believe it has value. They look for better ways to fit themselves into their jobs. They exercise their talents confidently and are more open to change. They support the enterprise because they feel the enterprise supports them.

The Structure of the Book

Driving Fear Out of the Workplace is structured to help readers accomplish this vision. The book has four parts. Part One is made up of the first two chapters and focuses on the dynamics of fear. Chapter One describes major themes that reappear throughout the book and gives a picture of what a quality organization can be like. Chapter Two summarizes the research work of others, describes our field study, and provides key definitions. In Part Two, Chapters Three through Six explore our research findings as a sequence of discoveries about how fear operates in organizations. Chapter Seven concludes the second section of the book with a description of a cycle that continues to feed fear and keep it alive in the workplace.

The third part of the book details strategies that build high-trust work environments. It begins, in Chapter Eight, with a vision for exceptional manager-employee relationships and an outline of the skills necessary to implement the strategies we suggest. Chapters Nine through Fifteen identify seven specific strategies, each broken into a number of action steps. The strategies and steps range from basic to complex, enabling readers to select the appropriate level and type of approach for their organization. Our final chapter in Part Four identifies ways to extend the previous strategies and highlights the long-term challenges and satisfactions that await managers committed to reducing fear.

What We Do Not Include

There are many areas that we would have liked to pursue, but of necessity some aspects have been left out. We hope that others will be sufficiently intrigued by our findings and suggestions to investigate additional facets of this topic. For example, we think the following questions deserve greater exploration:

- Are there differences between the way men and women view and react to fear? Does age—or proximity to retirement—make a difference?
- Can the study of fear help organizations deal more effectively with racism, sexism, and other types of discrimination?
- Is there a way to calculate the dollar-value costs of fear to organizations?
- What impact does organizational structure have on the amount of fear or trust present in a workplace?
- What is the full relationship between powerlessness and fear at work?
- What needs to happen so the "paradigm shift" of values and methods taking place in business can occur without frightening and alienating people?

These questions range from the practical to the philosophical. Some of them are not addressed because we do not know the answers. Others are explored briefly; however, we list them here because there is much more to learn from discussion and research.

In addition to these unanswered questions, we only lightly touch upon ways to influence the behavior of managers higher in the organization whose conduct is causing fear. Our strategies are worded to focus on what managers can do to reduce fear within the organizations that report to them, not within the reporting relationships above them. We have adopted this approach for several reasons:

- Our belief is that managers have the responsibility of initiating efforts to reduce fear.
- Influencing relationships with subordinates is often easier and faster than with superiors.
- In some instances, there is virtually nothing a subordinate can do to change a fear-oriented management style or work environment.
- One of the best methods of influencing higher levels of the system is by creating success stories at lower levels.

Although we have chosen not to work extensively with influencing higher levels directly, we believe that individuals interested in this problem can benefit from this book. They will have to think through ways in which the strategies could be adapted to their own situations. We address this concern briefly in our final chapter. We sense that while the strategies may not be radically different from those presented, it may take much longer to realize change.

Acknowledgments

We are particularly grateful to the 260 people across the country who talked to us about their experiences with fear. Without their help, our work would lack candor and the vitality of real life. In each organization we visited, there was at least one person who served as a logistical contact. These people went out of their way to assist us, sometimes taking a risk or two simply to set up interviews. Their willingness to take risks and their practical assistance made our fieldwork possible.

While writing this book we have been surrounded by supportive friends, colleagues, clients, and family members whose belief in us and enthusiasm for our work kept us on track. In many cases, with our clients in particular, these individuals consistently demonstrated management practice based on trust and collaboration and a willingness to deal with fear in a straightforward, courageous way. We have learned much from them.

There are a few individuals who must be thanked outright for their support. George Orr, Ryan's business partner and husband, conducted interviews, assisted with data analysis, did library research, and served as a third, less visible member of the team. More than once his diplomatic questions caused us to rethink an idea or refine our analysis. His ever-present support was a critical resource to us. Howard Strickler, personnel director for the City of Bellevue, Washington, created space and time for us to develop and finish our work. His love and respect for people and his outstanding managerial skills made him our favorite model of a great boss. The organization development scholars and practitioners associated with the Texas Rehabilitation Commission graciously shared with us the findings from their own research and practice. Geoffrey Bellman generously offered information, insight, and experience. His good name was the key that opened many doors for us—one of which led to Ray Bard, who managed the production of this book. Ray's knowledge of the publishing business and fine thinking sharpened our concepts and helped us make tangible the desire to write this book.

In a category of their own are our spouses, George Orr and Sarah Stiteler. Their unquestioned support, patience, and loving commitment will be remembered and treasured. We have learned through them that book writing—at least our version of it—is truly a family affair.

December, 1990   Kathleen D. Ryan
                                                     Bellevue, Washington

                                                     Daniel K. Oestreich
                                                     Redmond, Washington

THE AUTHORS

■

Kathleen D. Ryan is known for her work in team development, strategic planning, and continuous quality improvement. As a principal in the Orion Partnership, a consulting firm based in Bellevue, Washington, her practice focuses on clients in the service sector. In addition to her consulting work, Ryan serves as director of the Organization Development Professional Practice Area for the American Society for Training and Development. She received her B.A. degree (1969) in English from the University of California at Berkeley and her M.A. degree (1978) in public administration from the University of Southern California. In 1980, she co-produced the award-winning training film *The Workplace Hustle*. She has published on the topics of resistance to change, group process facilitation, sexual harassment, and peer pressure. Ryan is also a member of the Organizational Development Network.

Daniel K. Oestreich is principal of Oestreich Associates, a management and organization development consulting practice. He specializes in ways to build effective teams and frequently incorporates the principles of self-managing workteams and quality improvement into his work for public- and private-sector clients. His professional background includes many years as a personnel generalist for the City of Bellevue, Washington, where he worked "in the trenches" with many facets of employee selection, classification and pay, affirmative action, employee assistance, training, and organization development. He initiated the City's quality improvement effort, one of the first municipal efforts of its kind nationally. He graduated cum laude with a B.A. degree in history from Yale University in 1973 and in 1975 received an M.A. degree in guidance and counseling from the University of Colorado at Boulder. Oestreich is a member of the American Society for Training and Development and the American Society for Quality Control.

PART ONE

■

THE
DYNAMICS
OF
FEAR

1

HOW FEAR
PREVENTS PEOPLE
FROM DOING
THEIR BEST

When people hear
the word *fear* connected with the workplace, they think about it in many different ways: fear of change, fear of failure,
fear of the boss—to name only a few.
This book focuses on the fears people
have about speaking up at work. The fear
of speaking up can be thought of as a
composite of many types of workplace

anxieties, which together form a most basic human barrier to improving an organization. By examining what people are reluctant to speak up about and why, we have an opportunity to see how fear prevents people from doing their best at work. This is not just a problem of a few unassertive souls who lack confidence. Virtually all of us, at one time or another, have hesitated to talk about certain specific work-related issues. When that hesitation is linked to concern about personal negative consequences, we become victims of fear. Consider:

- The manager who feels frustrated by, but unable to talk about, the direct power a CEO exerts over personnel selection in his division

- The secretary who quietly resents the fact that she is really doing her boss's job

- The human resources specialist who cannot confront her supervisor's public negativity about changes and new initiatives

- The president of a subsidiary organization who resists, but does not openly confront, ineffective practices mandated by the corporate office

- The front-line manufacturing worker who hesitates to tell a new supervisor about practical ways to make the work go more smoothly

The fear behind these scenarios generates negativity, anger, and frustration. It depletes pride and undermines quality, productivity, and innovation. Because fear is an interactive process involving communication between at least two people, the dynamics of workplace relationships must be better understood. Thus, *Driving Fear Out of the Workplace* focuses on relationships and interpersonal communication—with an emphasis on what goes on between managers and their employees. A variety of work-related fears are explored, including:

- Having one's credibility questioned
- Being left out of decision making
- Being criticized in front of others
- Not getting information necessary to succeed
- Having a key assignment given to someone else
- Disagreements which might lead to damaged relationships
- Getting stuck in a dead-end job
- Not getting deserved recognition

- Not being seen as a team player
- Suggestions being misinterpreted as criticisms
- Poor levels of performance
- Getting fired

The ideas, theories, and suggestions we present come from three sources: the work of others who have studied and written about organizational behavior, our observations and experiences as consultants, and interviews we have conducted with a wide range of people across the United States. As we consolidated the data from our interviews, four interrelated themes began to appear. These cut across much of the material we present in this book.

KEY THEMES

The Relationship with the Boss Is of Key Importance

As one person succinctly put it, "It all depends on who you're working for." A marketing person in a large telecommunications company told us, "My boss makes the difference. If I don't have someone I can trust, I get angry and scared and my work quality is lowered. People need a climate where they can grow." A district manager in the same organization said that he was lucky—he trusted and respected both his boss and his boss's boss. Reflecting on past experiences, he allowed, "I'm more hesitant to give bad news to some than to others. Some just go critical, rather than going forward." From a more cynical perspective, a second-level manager at a Fortune 100 company commented, "Some bosses are better than others. If they react without thinking, you can't trust them. Very few set the right environment."

In interview after interview, the pattern was the same, regardless of the level of the person being interviewed. The quality of the relationship a person has with his or her direct supervisor is a key determinant of the fear—or lack of fear—that person experiences at work. Typically, people talked to us about their one-on-one relationships. But frequently, we would hear "us and them" references which indicated that fear exists as a broad pattern between hierarchical levels.

One reason the relationship with the immediate boss emerged as an important theme is that the past is still with us. Within the traditional hierarchical organization, the boss always ran the show. What he—

and in this traditional world we do mean *he*—wanted, he got. As one seasoned retiree we know puts it, the job of an employee was to "find out what the old boy wants and give it to him." The boss—not the customer—was always right and set the party line. And if the boss did not get what he wanted, the employee would pay, just like Dagwood and Mr. Dithers. Bosses hired "hands" to do a job. While common sense and rational thinking ability were important, employees were not expected to voice opinions or feelings about what they saw happening in their organizations. The workplace was supposed to be systematic, efficient, and rational. It was not a place to be cluttered up by employee interests, viewpoints, or emotions.

The working world of the 1990s is a different place. But the legacy of fear and mistrust associated with traditional hierarchies is still part of the background noise in most organizations. To free our organizations from outdated and stereotypic management practices, people in management positions must take the lead. While they need the cooperation of their employees to be successful, it is management's job to begin the change.

A Little Bit of Fear Goes a Long Way

At least 70 percent of the 260 people we interviewed said that they had hesitated to speak up because they feared some type of repercussion. While we know that some managers consciously intimidate their employees, most do not. We are confident that the greatest percentage of intimidating behaviors are committed unconsciously by managers who have no idea how their behavior is affecting others. Moreover, given the legacy of mistrust from traditional hierarchies, many employees expect to experience repercussions even though there may be no immediate evidence that they actually will occur. These two factors continually lead to misunderstandings and distance between people.

Since this book is written for managers, we focus our attention on what managers say and do, often unthinkingly, that may cause employees to worry about repercussions. As one manager said, "No one tries to manage by fear. Our behavior is avoidance for the most part and people become afraid because of it." Another interpretation of the same dilemma came from a dock worker who observed that "some of the worst offenders in terms of fear are the ones who don't know they do it." Because of the mistrust that typically exists between hierarchical levels, the impact of intimidation that does happen to employees is magnified. A little bit can go a long way. Small interactions, never intended to be very important, take on greater, sometimes symbolic, proportions. Like pollution in water, their effect can spread fast and far.

While it is hard work, we know that it is very possible to turn the cycles of fear and mistrust around and to tap the underutilized potential of every organization. As many of our strategies suggest, talking about fear—saying it out loud—is a powerful way to begin. This simple action goes a long way to repair damaged relationships and counteract the negative expectations that have carried over from traditional hierarchies. Fear of speaking up has been around and ignored for so long that addressing it directly is a dramatic and visible way to break new ground. Our suggestions encourage managers to communicate with the honest philosophy: "We're going to talk about what's going on here. We're no longer going to ignore how people really feel." For some managers this philosophy may represent a very different way of doing business.

When Threatened, People React with Strong Emotions

The fantasy about organizational life is that people will behave in logical, unemotional, and well-organized ways. It is as though the boxes on the organization charts are designed to keep the messiness of reality, people, and emotions away from work. If anything, our interviews have confirmed that the messiness is largely inescapable. People are not objective about their jobs; they take their work very personally. Their feelings cannot be separated from their productivity and the quality of their work. When they cannot do the right thing or do a good job, it bothers them a great deal. And when the fear of repercussions is a barrier to quality work, their emotions are strong ones—as the following statements reveal.

66 *If you experience fear every day, it drags you down and you become cowardly.* 99
> **—Hospital phlebotomist**

66 *I'd rather go someplace else, make less money, and feel better about myself.* 99
> **—Career manager,**
> **Fortune 100 company**

66 *After my suggestions were ignored, the quality of my work was still there, but I wasn't.* 99
> **—Internal consultant**
> **in a bank**

66 *In retrospect, I felt like a battered wife. I wasn't allowed to talk with anyone.* 99
> **—Personnel manager,**
> **major U.S. corporation**

When we asked people to tell us about the impact of the situations in which they did not speak up, they talked to us much more about what they *felt* than what they *thought*. Sixty percent of their responses involved strong negative emotions. To many people, there was no question that their damaged feelings had a negative effect on the quality, amount, or efficiency of their work. People made mistakes, refused to bring up key issues, or could not be creative because of working in a fear-oriented environment. For many, the inability to do their best work was inseparable from the way fear made them feel about themselves and their organization.

In Spite of Fear, Most Organizations Operate Satisfactorily

Given the topic of this book, it could be assumed that we think things are in a bigger mess than they really are. On the contrary, of the twenty-two organizations we visited, none was on the brink of disaster. Many were grappling with the challenges of increased competition and rising costs. Among them there had been mergers, reorganizations, and layoffs. But on the average, our sample organizations would be regarded as moderately successful or better. Many were on the path of improvement. Some were realizing significant success.

We see the presence of fear as an undertone, a less-than-obvious influence that keeps both individuals and their organizations from being fully effective. Fear in the workplace detracts from organizational success. It represents lost opportunities to realize untapped potential.

The dynamics are not unlike those connected with individual fitness. Fear is like tobacco to the one-pack-a-day smoker. It slows down organizations the way smoking slows down people. It limits their capacity. It keeps them from being peak competitors. It counteracts many other productive habits and routines. The metaphor presents an obvious question for organizations and their managers: "Is it worth it?"

ACHIEVING A VISION OF QUALITY, PRODUCTIVITY, AND INNOVATION

The point about organizations operating satisfactorily is an important one. It means that at a minimum, diminishing fear can be viewed as an enhancement, not an overhaul. At a deeper level, however, reducing fear is an essential component of organizational transformation. In subtle ways this effort changes the underlying characteristics of the whole organization, thereby liberating it to achieve, in new ways, a vision of quality, productivity, and innovation. Reducing fear and increasing trust help people to reconsider their organization's possibilities and to step outside the box of existing methods. People can then develop faith that their vision for a quality organization really can be attained.

Our idea of this vision is not unique in itself. It is similar to ideas found in many management books and corporate philosophy statements. The quality organization

- Produces high-quality goods and services that more than meet the needs of loyal, satisfied customers
- Is a great place to work—employees at all levels feel proud of their work and their organization
- Respects employees for their competence, perspectives, and contributions
- Encourages and supports leadership at all levels
- Is characterized by openness, competence, and high ethical standards
- Celebrates a shared purpose and appreciates the interdependence between levels and functions

To these characteristics we would also add the notion that quality organizations are not utopias. They face plenty of problems and conflicts. But when problems do come up, managers and employees throughout the organization approach them with a positive, non-blaming, data-based perspective. The motivation is to solve the problem and eliminate the barrier—not to point fingers or place blame. There is freedom to openly disagree, to consider all relevant information, and to challenge the status quo without defensiveness. Mistakes are acknowledged and people are supported based on their intentions or their search for information, new approaches, or improvements.

Most importantly, manager-employee relationships are based on trust, respect, and mutual credibility. Positive intentions are assumed. When either person is confused or frustrated by the other's action, the response is one of curiosity and a desire for information, rather than suspicion and a need to find fault. What fear exists is not the fear of repercussions, but the self-imposed tension that comes from wanting to meet high personal standards.

Throughout this book, we often juxtapose the challenge of reducing fear with the desire to achieve a vision of quality, productivity, and innovation. The first addresses the dark, unpleasant, harsh side of work. The second pulls people forward to a lofty, inspired, and fulfilling future. The difference between the two can trigger a disquieting question: What can managers do to bridge a gulf that seems so deep? Our generalized answer to this question is: Go slowly; work on one problem at a time; follow a philosophy of continuous, incremental improvement rather than rapid quantum leaps; and initiate positive action to build trust at the same time that efforts are made to reduce fear. Our strategy chapters provide specific guidance about how to do this.

We start, however, with the real world of messy, ineffective human interaction. The research findings we present and the stories we tell in the next six chapters are discouraging. They indict managers and employees alike. They call attention to the collective imperfections, foolishness, and self-centeredness of those of us who work in organizations. They acknowledge a world where people resist change, where skills are underdeveloped, where historical bad blood and internal politics keep people at odds with each other. We ask for our readers' forbearance in working with this material. We believe that unless managers understand the powerful, hidden, and unexplored aspects of fear in the workplace, they will not be fully prepared to provide the leadership necessary to establish the vision. Perhaps, at this point in the management literature, this is the unique contribution we can make with this book.

The news is by no means all bad. As we have pointed out, most of the organizations with which we have had contact are doing moderately well. And there is a wealth of evidence demonstrating that positive changes are occurring all around us. Business journals are full of positive developments that come from quality improvement, self-managing work teams, and renewed dedication to customer service.

To us the changes that best reflect the vision of the quality organization are found in the experiences of individuals. We have seen repeated illustrations in the organizations our clients manage and in examples we discovered through our interviews. Consider the following stories.

THREE CASES

In the Atlanta area we met a woman in her late twenties holding a technical position within a small manufacturing company. Starting as a mail clerk, she had been with the company for ten years, during which time she had gone to night school to finish her degree. When we asked her if there was a situation in which she had hesitated to speak up, she told us about one that had happened recently, just after she had received a new promotion.

> 66 I was given a project by myself. I was told that I would be given help on the area I was less familiar with. When I got to that part, the resources were not available. I spent a week floundering. I was afraid to say anything—afraid that one day I might report to one of these people who would remember I couldn't do anything.

> 66 Finally, I said something to my manager. He arranged a meeting for me with the other managers involved and a vice-president. I went in ready to defend myself, but they listened and gave me the help I needed. I was really surprised. In the future, I don't think I'll wait so long. I'll raise the flag right away. 99

In St. Louis, at a large communications firm, we talked with a senior-level manager who sang the praises of his boss, a senior vice-president. He said that he currently did not have to worry about speaking up. When asked about the behaviors his boss exhibited that made it easy for him to voice his concerns, he gave us the following list.

> 66 He won't hold things against me. He won't talk negatively to others about me. There is a type of intangible trust between us. And it's not that he's just a nice guy—he follows up on what he says. He asks for my opinion and encourages me to speak out. He usually supports my position but lets me know when he can't. He goes out of his way to acknowledge my good ideas, giving me the credit for my ideas when he's talking to his boss. He's flexible enough to try for compromise, even when he doesn't have to. 99

He then reflected that if his boss's style "was practiced by more senior managers, much of this discussion about fear would be put aside."

Finally, in Rochester, New York, a manager in a large corporation talked to us about his decision to start acting in a more assertive, risk-taking fashion. He began his interview by saying, "I see so many people asking permission to do their jobs. I've stopped asking permission and have not gotten in trouble." He reflected that when he approached his twenty-year anniversary with the company, he realized that "I'd never felt the same satisfaction with my work life that I'd felt with my family. I felt cheated to think that I would not end my career with my head held high." He decided to change that.

> 66 *I now assume a level of equality, and I see others' trust and confidence in me grow. I've begun to treat my folks as I want to be treated: I promote our collective success. My most important job is to represent the best interests of my employees. I've become more sensitive to the fact that I'm a role model.* 99

When asked about the impact of his new, bolder approach, he said,

> 66 *I get fewer directives because I've become unafraid to disagree, to say no. People see me now as an honest broker of services. I got a bonus and experience a much greater sense of success. I think I get 20 percent more out of the same investment.* 99

Twenty percent is not a shabby return. Examples such as these support our fundamental optimism: The vision of the quality organization can be achieved. Not overnight and not all at once. Starting perhaps with smaller organizations first, or in units or sections of larger corporations. Or perhaps in a single relationship between a supervisor and an employee. Whenever people take action to reduce fear, the quality organization becomes a more probable future.

2

THE
BOUNDARIES
OF FEAR

This chapter has three components which, woven together, provide support for the information and suggestions we present in coming chapters. These three objectives are (1) outlining the research and theories of others who have linked fear to work environments, (2) describing our own field study methodology and sample, and (3) presenting and illustrating the definition of fear in the workplace used throughout this book.

WHAT OTHERS HAVE SAID ABOUT FEAR

Our readings focused on the fields of psychology, education, the social sciences, and business, including the literature on quality. While we found many references to fear, trust, the organizational climate, and the supervisor-subordinate relationship, no one major work directly addressed the specific topic of our exploration. We have continued to find very little information about the fears that keep people from speaking up at work. We summarize here a handful of interrelated works which provide a foundation and several reference points for our study. Together they highlight the relationships between fear, trust, and mistrust; breakdowns in interpersonal communication; and organizational ineffectiveness.

From the psychological literature, S. J. Rachman's work *Fear and Courage* (1978, pp. 7–10) has been helpful to us. He provides a straightforward definition of fear as "the experience of apprehension" and cites four major causes:

- Exposure to traumatic stimulation
- Repeated exposures to subtraumatic sensitizing situations
- Observations, direct or indirect, of people exhibiting fear
- Transmission of fear-inducing information

Rachman observes that "fears can be acquired vicariously or by direct transmission of information." "Controllability" is a key element from his perspective. He defines it as a sense of whether or not one "is in a position to reduce the likelihood of an adverse event and/or its consequences." He adds: "If in the face of threats, we feel unable to control the probable outcome, we are likely to experience fear." He also finds that "behavior or information that increases one's predictability is likely to contribute to a reduction in fear."

In the mid-1960s both Douglas McGregor and Jack Gibb wrote about fear within organizations. In *The Professional Manager,* McGregor remarked that effective organizations require open, authentic communications. These, in turn, depend upon "a climate of mutual trust and support with the group. In such a climate, members can be themselves without fearing the consequences" (1967, p. 192). In his classic articles on defensive management and communication, Jack Gibb talks quite specifically about a fear-distrust cycle and the patterns that keep people's interaction at work defensive rather than participative (1961, 1965).

Gibb's fear-distrust cycle, which appears throughout much of his work, is one where "a self-fulfilling prophecy ensues: low-trust, high-fear theories generate more fear and distrust" (1978, p. 192). He builds the case that fear is the opposite of trust and that fear and distrust always go together. Throughout his book *Trust,* he contrasts the behavior and thinking patterns that are based on defensiveness and fear to those oriented around trust. It is as though he was warning the organizations of the 1990s when he identified the circumstances in which defensiveness is most likely to appear: "This vicious defense cycle occurs in organizations particularly when fears are high and at times of emergencies, poor market conditions, pressure from top management, cultural unrest, labor pressures, heightened ambiguity, or massive change of any kind" (1978, p. 192). He writes that the cycle "spirals and feeds upon itself" and "builds a general climate of constraint; creates dependent, passive and conforming people, and brings such people into positions of visibility and influence—the Peter principle; and sets up forces and organizational structures that sustain the fear defense" (1978, p. 192).

The impact of such dynamics on organizational effectiveness was further documented by Dale Zand. In 1972, he observed that people who do not trust each other will distort information in an effort to protect themselves. In the workplace this results in information that is "low in accuracy, comprehensiveness, and timeliness." The non-trusting person will also "resist or deflect the attempts of others to exert influence. He will be suspicious of their views and not receptive to their proposals of goals, their suggestions for reaching goals, and their definition of criteria and methods for evaluating success." He adds: "All this behavior, following from a lack of trust, will be deleterious to information exchange, to reciprocity of influence, and the exercise of self-control, and will diminish the effectiveness of joint problem-solving efforts" (1972, p. 230).

Adding to the theory that threats and mistrust have a negative impact on organizational effectiveness is Chris Argyris. In the mid-1980s, he described groups of highly skilled communicators who, in their efforts to avoid conflict and upset, did not talk about issues that are critical for organizational problem solving. Such "skilled incompetence" is maintained by the "defensive routines" which represent "any action or policy designed to avoid surprise, embarrassment, or threat." The negative impact on problem solving is unintended. Nonetheless, these behaviors "prevent learning and thereby prevent organizations from investigating or eliminating" their underlying problems (1986, pp. 75–76). Argyris claims that the only way these defensive routines can be broken is for people to talk to each other about their suspicions and mistrust—breaking a pattern of what he calls "undiscussability." Like Zand, Argyris and his colleagues find that "human beings, when dealing with threatening issues, typically act in ways that inhibit the generation of valid information and that create self-sealing patterns of escalating error." They see people withholding thoughts and feelings, speaking with high levels of inference, attributing defensiveness and negative motives to others, and placing the responsibility for errors on others or situational factors (Argyris, Putnam, and Smith, 1985, pp. 61–62).

Peter Block picks up this pattern of dependent behavior in *The Empowered Manager* when he describes what he calls a "bureaucratic cycle." The requirements of the patriarchal contract—which is at the heart of bureaucratic behavior—are that employees:

- Submit to authority
- Deny self-expression
- Sacrifice for unnamed future rewards
- Believe that these requirements are just

He illuminates the chilling cost for organizations when they operate with such tacit agreements:

> The price the organization pays for giving such emphasis to authority is the feeling of helplessness it creates. If it's not my fault, I can't fix it. This is the collusion between the management and the people working for them. Managers take comfort in the fact that there are people under their control who are forced to submit to their wishes, and this gives them the illusion of power and influence.

> Subordinates take comfort in the fact that when things go wrong, it is not their fault; and the fact that they pay for this comfort with their own helplessness is a small price to pay [1987, p. 26].

At the base of such dependent behavior—for both management and employees—is an "us and them" mindset which says that "if people are left to their own instincts and their own authority, they'll somehow act in a way that runs counter to society and counter to the organization. We fear that people basically do not have the wish or the ability to act responsibly and that external authority must be constantly reinforced in order to keep us focused on common goals for the common purpose" (1987, p. 29).

In *The Abilene Paradox,* Jerry Harvey presents the idea that the judgmental way of thinking described by Block is not what really causes people to be suspicious, to be unwilling to take risks, or to withdraw from responsibility. He suggests that an instinctive fear of separation from others causes people to say and do things that will elicit approval from others. With everyone acting this way at once and with people focusing on the ways in which they are different from everyone else, few people recognize that they really are after the same goals. He comments: "The fear of taking risks that may result in our separation from others is at the core of the paradox. It finds expression in ways of which we may be unaware, and it is ultimately the cause of the self-defeating, collective deception that leads to self-destructive decisions within organizations" (1988, p. 24).

He agrees with Alvin Toffler and Phillip Slater, who "contend that our cultural emphasis on technology, competition, individualism, temporariness, and mobility has resulted in a population that has frequently experienced the terror of loneliness and seldom the satisfaction of engagement. Consequently, though we have learned the reality of separation, we have not had the opportunity to learn the skills of connection" (Harvey, 1988, p. 25).

All of these authors pay attention to what needs to be done to turn around the negative patterns and cycles they describe. Their suggestions vary, but they all offer strategies which support an environment of greater trust and risk taking and a decrease in fear and mistrust. We have found their theories enlightening and generally consistent with our own recommendations. In the pages that follow, many of our concepts have obvious links to their work.

Rachman's four causes of fear are similar to those we describe as *sources of threat* later in this chapter. His ideas also are connected to our view that people's fears can be actual, perceived, or imagined. His points about controllability and predictability are reflected in our strategy chapters on decision making and ambiguous behaviors. Gibb and Zand both offer cycles that relate to the cycle of mistrust we describe in Chapter Seven. Argyris's notion of undiscussability significantly influenced our use of the term "undiscussables" to describe the issues that people do not talk about. The ideas of Block and Harvey are confirmed by many of the themes from our field research and, in a background manner, guide many of the actions we suggest in our strategy chapters.

W. Edwards Deming's references to fear in *Out of the Crisis* (1986, pp. 59–62) have served as the catalyst for others, like ourselves, who see it as a most significant barrier to quality, productivity, and innovation. In his overview of the steps necessary to transform American organizations, he briefly lists the types of fears typically experienced: job loss, poor performance, limited career options, loss of personal credibility, and lack of trust of management. With "Drive Out Fear"

(p. 59), Deming provides a provocative challenge, but does not offer much specific guidance about *how* to reduce fear in the workplace.

Two works stand as important elaborations of Deming's ideas. William Scherkenbach in *The Deming Route to Quality and Productivity* parallels some of our work by describing a fear-oriented cycle that begins with top managers only wanting to hear good news. The "kill the messenger" syndrome results in filtered information from those lower in the hierarchy. In turn, this leads to micromanagement and attempts to set up sophisticated information systems that bypass mistrusted middle managers. As a result, fear is increased and there is an even greater tendency to kill the messenger. He also points out that, ironically, fear can lead to greater communication when employees band together to represent an image of teamwork to those higher up in the system. It can lead to dysfunctional agreements such as, "If you don't mess in my nest, I won't mess in yours" (1986, pp. 71, 76).

Howard Gitlow and Shelly Gitlow in *The Deming Guide to Quality and Competitive Position* mirror views we heard frequently from those participating in our field research. For example, they comment;

> Managers want to deny that people have problems and fears. They walk around with blinders, trying to attend to their "managerial duties." They are able to keep their distance from workers because of the absorbing layers of middle management, whose job is keeping a lid on problems. What these managers are ignoring is that their job *is* dealing with employees' problems, eliminating their fears, and encouraging the development of people. Human beings have emotions that strongly influence their behavior. Their fears are a barrier to their emotional well-being and their job performance. Managers have to relate to employees on a person-to-person basis. . . . After all, managers have experienced the same fears and should be able to communicate this to their subordinates [1987, pp. 137–138].

The Gitlows quote a private conversation with Dr. Deming that strikes at the heart of the problem. They report that Deming felt "the fundamental problem in American business is that people are scared to discuss the problems of people" (1987, p. 137).

The most recent effort, and the one which comes closest to our emphasis, is a 1989 journal article by Theodore Lowe and Gerald McBean. They define six "monsters of fear": fear of reprisal, failure, providing information, not knowing, giving up control, and change (1989). While ours is a more extensive treatment of the subject matter, we touch on many of the same issues.

ABOUT OUR FIELD RESEARCH

Together with a third colleague, George Orr, we interviewed 260 people in a broad spectrum of organizations—twenty-two altogether, evenly divided between service and manufacturing sectors with government included. Our geographic spread included the areas surrounding Atlanta; Chicago; St. Louis; Rochester, New York; San Francisco; Austin, Texas; and Seattle. We talked to people at all levels, from CEOs to mechanics. While we do not claim this to be a rigorous sample, the information these individuals provided to us is highly suggestive. During the course of our sixty- to ninety-minute standardized interviews, we asked four basic questions:

- What issues have you hesitated to talk about at work in the last five years of your job experience?

- Why didn't you talk about them?

- Did you hesitate to speak up on an issue because you feared some type of repercussion?

- What were those threatening situations and what impact did they have?

The results of our interviews have been consolidated according to broad categories. This was accomplished by counting the number of times particular topics, responses, or comments surfaced during the interview discussions. We did our best to balance the different levels of participation of those interviewed and the different questioning styles of the interviewers. When in doubt, we always opted for the more conservative interpretation of what people said: We did not presume fear to exist when it was not obvious.

We have woven into our chapters the answers to these questions along with relevant consulting experience. All references to organizations or individuals are disguised. We made this pledge of anonymity in order to make those we interviewed feel comfortable talking about their experiences. Individuals usually were selected by an internal coordinator or contact person. This was done in no particular manner and often depended on who had time on their calendars on the days we were in town. We specifically asked that people *not* be selected because they might have some special experience related to fear. Other than that, we made no effort to control the makeup of our sample. The numbers fell into the categories shown in Table 1.

TABLE 1
Research Sample

Category	No.	Percentage of Responses
Level of position		
CEOs	4	1
Senior managers	16	6
Mid-level managers	62	24
Professional staff (do not supervise)	53	20
First-level supervisors	25	10
Front-line staff		
Technical/paraprofessional	47	18
Clerical	35	14
Blue collar	18	7
Total	260	100
Number of people by race/gender		
White males	98	38
White females	123	47
Men of color	16	6
Women of color	23	9
Total	260	100
Participating organizations		
Service	9	41
Government	3	14
Manufacturing	10	45
Total	22	100
Size of organizations		
Over 10,000 employees	10	46
Between 2,000 and 10,000 employees	6	27
Fewer than 2,000 employees	6	27
Total	22	100

As a result of this effort, we can quantify the number of people who report particular aspects of their work experience. We can list and categorize their concerns and the behaviors they view as threatening. No matter how much we would like to be able to do so, we cannot quantify the cost of fear to organizations or individuals or the exact impact of the turn-around strategies we suggest. In these areas, we offer our best professional judgment about what is needed and what will work to overcome the patterns of fear.

OUR DEFINITIONS

We define fear in the workplace as *feeling threatened by possible repercussions as a result of speaking up about work-related concerns.* These feelings of threat can come from four sources:

- Actual experience in the current situation, or in a past similar situation

- Stories about others' experiences

- Assumptions and private interpretations of others' behaviors

- Negative, culturally based stereotypes about those with supervisory power

Any given situation can reflect one or more of these sources. Consider the following example provided by a first-level manager in a mid-sized service organization.

66 When my supervisor's boss started some years ago, I was afraid for my job. He changed things without talking to the managers. He put people down. He would ask a question and if you didn't immediately know the answer, he would say something like, 'Well, you obviously don't know about such and such'—he would challenge your competence.

66 He would kid people a lot, but it felt like he wasn't really kidding. To a friend of his in the organization he referred to me as 'the resident female chauvinist.' Another woman said he referred to her as 'the baby factory.' He gave my supervisor a hard time about where he went to college, that sort of thing. He exudes confidence, but I really think it's not true—he's really not that confident. It's always important to let him feel like 'Mr. Big Guy.'

> ❝ *Not long after he was appointed, he decided we should go on a team-building retreat. Everybody was required to go. There was an insinuation that if you wanted your job, you'd better go. Throughout the four days of the retreat there was a real undercurrent. An agenda had been sent out, but we didn't know what it meant. It had things like 'blind walk' and 'electric fence' on it. We were all in such a state, but we didn't feel we could do anything about it. The retreat resulted in us developing a common enemy—him. It forged a commitment among us to operate the firm in spite of him—a commitment to each other.*
>
> ❝ *In my last appraisal, I was written up for being outspoken. My supervisor wrote, 'It's not a problem for me or the new boss, but somebody from the outside who doesn't know you might not think it appropriate.' Fear of reprisal is a big deal around here because 'partnership' has been rammed at us, yet fear persists because it really means, 'We only want team players.'* ❞

As with many organizations, *team player* in this manager's work environment is interpreted as someone who does not criticize the boss or the boss's decisions, and who supports the party line.

The example illustrates how the four sources of threat can easily become entangled and add to one another:

1. *Actual events.* The manager experiences being put down by her supervisor's boss and observes him putting others down with sarcastic comments and insinuations. She has a variety of reinforcing experiences at the team-building retreat. Her supervisor attempts to explain the reasons why being outspoken represents a performance problem.
2. *Experience of others.* A co-worker also experiences a sexist remark from the new boss.
3. *Assumptions.* The manager assumes that her supervisor's boss is emotionally insecure, that reprisals will take place if he is not made to feel "like Mr. Big Guy." She believes that her immediate supervisor is also afraid of the boss or is going along with him at her expense.
4. *Cultural stereotypes.* The manager and her co-workers banded together, for the sake of the organization, to overcome the boss who became a common enemy. This Hollywood-like scenario reflects strong cultural messages of the "little people" joining forces to counter the mean-spirited and more powerful boss.

We have come to believe that the mutually reinforcing effects of reality, stories, assumptions, and cultural stereotypes are what make fear at work so powerful. It does not really matter where the feelings of threat start, whether they are based on fact or fancy or some combination of the two. What is important is that they exist and that they keep people from taking initiatives and being fully productive. In the case of the first-level manager we interviewed, all of these factors blended to create real anxiety about losing her job.

She also reported the following effects of her fears:

> 66 *During that time I didn't do a whole lot of anything that was new or different. If an idea had come from one of my people, I would have accepted it and gone with it, but if it had come from above I would have evaluated it doubly because of the trust factor. I felt frustrated. My self-esteem was low and it showed. My relationships were more tense. I was quicker to fly off the handle, at work and at home. Now I've gotten to the point where I just blow it off. If I have a fear, it is of frustration—am I just spinning my wheels?* 99

As these words indicate, effects may not be directly quantifiable, but they are nonetheless alarming. When a first-level manager feels serious frustration, anger, mistrust, and futility, it is bound to influence the work group's performance as well as the manager's. Others we have talked with who experience these same feelings do *only* what it takes to survive and comply, and no more. They do not actively support upper-management decisions that remind them of the threats they feel themselves.

For example, our interview with this particular manager started with a discussion of a new performance appraisal system she was expected to implement. She described the system as requiring her to evaluate "attitude, loyalty, commitment to the firm." She told us how much she resented the new system, how it had been imposed by upper management with the attitude, "We're the bosses. We can evaluate anything we want to." She explained that this controlling mindset seemed to permeate the organization. She told us that management's attitude was "We should be able to tell people what to do and not have any problems with them." Resentment of the new appraisal system was similarly expressed to us by her subordinates.

Her story raises uncomfortable questions:

- Was her supervisor's boss as bad as he seemed?
- What were the intentions behind the team-building retreat?
- How did others feel about this event?
- What were upper management's real intentions in implementing a new appraisal system?
- Is the first-level manager simply a resister, unaccepting of top management's legitimate prerogatives?

We do not know the answers to these questions. We do know that for those hearing the story as it is presented here, taking sides, offering interpretations, or finding fault with the bosses or the employee would be an easy but unfortunate response. We believe that the best way to view this story is as an example of how fear becomes deeply woven into the whole fabric of an organization, how it can lead *both* managers and employees to play unproductive roles. To change such a system requires a broad effort in which everyone is involved and does his or her part.

LIMITS OF THE TOPIC

Our definition of fear at work does have clear limits. We exclude:

- Tension that emanates from the work itself—that is, the stress that normally comes from working with reasonable deadlines, handling sensitive encounters with customers, dealing with new information or technologies, and other job-related causes

- Fear of a particular task, such as public speaking

- Situations where someone is unnecessarily anxious or suspicious over "what might happen" in an environment where trust is generally high and communication is open

- Anxieties that are the result of unrealistic personal standards

- Fears associated with appropriately administered disciplinary action

In other words, we attempt to exclude *fears over which the organization has no meaningful control.* Our definition focuses on what most people experience in their working lives; it does not emphasize situations where special support is required.

DEFINITIONAL "YES-BUTS"

There are some fears which on the surface seem to be excluded from our definition. Further reflection shows that they are sometimes prime examples of fear at work. Discipline, for example, is a concept that raises "yes-buts" about the fear of speaking up. In certain circumstances, a supervisor may claim that she or he was left "no choice" in imposing a particular disciplinary action—or even that it was to the employee's overall benefit—when in fact the corrective action was a form of reprisal. In one organization, managers admitted that some internal transfers of employees were actually punishment for having challenged the decisions of the top executive. But in each case there was also a conveniently humane business reason for the transfer, such as "career development of the employee" or "cross-training." Because the employees knew the real reasons behind the transfers, this practice caused enormous mistrust and perpetuated tremendous fear within the organization.

Similarly, some dismiss others' fears of repercussions as a sign of personal insecurities. This is a convenient way to stamp out further discussion or criticism of actual management practices by subordinates. Because of our culture's myths and traditions of "rugged individualism," people who express their fears can be labeled as immature, cowardly, or overly emotional. Thus, to suggest that someone else is fearful can be an extremely powerful form of retaliation in itself. In effect, those who complain about fear-oriented management practices risk being labeled as insecure or weak. This double-bind traps people in "damned if you do, damned if you don't" thinking and prevents them from taking the most basic steps toward reducing fear at work.

REFINING THE DEFINITION

We chose the word *repercussions* to describe the wide range of things people are afraid of when they hesitate to speak up. It is a word selected with care. In our interviews, people used many terms. Along with *repercussions,* they told us about *retaliation, reprisals, retribution,* and *negative consequences.* These words did not necessarily correspond with the severity of their stories. For example, one person used *retaliation* to describe a supervisor who had forgotten an important piece of information; the employee saw this as an intentional act. Yet another thought *retaliation* too strong for a situation involving an immediate threat of physical violence. People used *any* of the words listed here to describe effects that ranged from subtle to dramatic, irritating to devastating.

We chose *repercussions* because it represents a reasonable midpoint. *Retaliation* and *reprisals* suggest intentional punishment or revenge. In fact, if our experiences are representative, people rarely plan to "get someone back" or "make so-and-so pay." Among all the stories we heard, only a very small number reflected possible conscious manipulation or abuse. On the other hand, a term such as *negative consequences* is overly neutral and does not connote the sense of being singled out. When we tried out a variety of words with some of our interview focus groups, *repercussions* invariably was the top choice to convey participants' experiences.

PRESENTATION OF RESEARCH DATA

The next five chapters outline the dynamics of the fear of speaking up and are illustrated by many stories and quotations gained through our research and consulting work. We encourage our readers to look for similarities between themselves and their organizations and the illustrations we present. If these personal connections do not happen, we suggest that the material be used as an observation point from which to better understand what others might experience. A recent interaction demonstrated how this can be helpful.

Not long ago, we were having a conversation with one of the individuals who reviewed an early draft of some of our chapters. He told us that when he first read our material, it made sense on a theoretical level, but he had a hard time relating to it personally. However, he had recently encountered a situation at work where the material had been very helpful.

He was asked to get involved in a situation where an employee of one of his subordinates was raising concerns about things that were happening at work. At first he judged her complaints to be irrational and paranoid and was inclined to dismiss them. Fortunately he remembered our chapters and began to see that the employee's concerns "might have a kernel of truth to them after all." It turned out that when our reviewer assumed his current managerial responsibilities, one of his first tasks was to terminate an employee for cause. That person just happened to be a friend of the woman who was now voicing concerns. As she told her story, he could see that from her viewpoint, worries about possible repercussions could make sense. This mind-shift enabled him to take a more respectful and open-minded view of the employee's concerns and function as a more constructive problem solver.

We hope our readers will benefit equally from what we have learned through our research and what we present in the next five chapters.

PART TWO

■

HOW
FEAR
OPERATES
IN
ORGANIZATIONS

3

UNDISCUSSABLES: SECRETS THAT EVERYONE KNOWS

A new manager who worked for a well-respected manufacturing firm was aware that several of his employees had complaints about how the operation had been going. He knew this because they had talked to him individually about their concerns. He made a point of bringing up these complaints at a staff meeting, believing that people would appreciate the chance to discuss and resolve some of them. To his great surprise, when he raised the issues there was dead silence. People would not talk openly about what they had privately expressed. The manager—and his group—had run into a brick wall of undiscussable issues.

The result was predictable. The manager was frustrated and mystified by his staff members' reaction. Resolution of problems in the operation were delayed because people would not talk about them. Those who were worried about the problems continued to be troubled with operational difficulties. We can only assume that these unsolved problems resulted in wasted time and money.

WHAT IS AN UNDISCUSSABLE?

As mentioned in the previous chapter, the concept of undiscussables reflects the work of Harvard educator Chris Argyris (Argyris, 1986; Argyris, Putnam, and Smith, 1985). While he uses "undiscussable" to describe defensive routines people exhibit in the work environment, we use this term to name the issues people are afraid to discuss. We define two components of an undiscussable, as it relates to issues of fear in the workplace. First, it is *a problem or issue that someone hesitates to talk about with those who are essential to its resolution.* Second, the fact that it is not discussed represents *a potential barrier to doing quality work or building an effective work relationship.*

Undiscussables are not talked about in the settings where they can be explored, explained, or resolved. They are the secrets that almost everyone knows about. The longer they remain undiscussed in the appropriate forums, the more they contribute to a climate of fear within the work environment. And the longer they remain undiscussed, the harder it becomes to talk about them. They are at the same time both a cause and a result of fear.

In spite of what our definition might imply, people *do* talk about undiscussables. Sometimes a lot. They are discussed privately, in the halls and bathrooms, over lunch or after work, during breaks at meetings, and on the job when other work should be attended to. They are discussed between friends, family members, and co-workers. If an employee has an undiscussable issue concerning a co-worker, it may get talked about with another peer or the employee's supervisor. Rumor mills exist almost solely to accommodate undiscussable issues.

WHAT PEOPLE ARE NOT
TALKING ABOUT

This chapter describes the wide range of issues people do not talk about and their patterns. Chapter Four will then explore the reasons why people do not speak up. We have come to view undiscussables as the window through which it is possible to see the dynamics that frighten people at work. Understanding undiscussables begins to lay the groundwork for strategies that can turn a fearful work climate into one characterized by risk taking and innovation. Table 2 summarizes the types of undiscussable issues identified by those we interviewed.

"Management practice" is by far the largest category of undiscussables. It includes a variety of issues related to how managers behave. People commented generally about managerial performance, about the technical competence of their bosses, and about the way in which their superiors managed people. Skill in "people management" was the item most often mentioned. Heavily influenced by perceptions of interpersonal communication, this area describes how managers interact with and provide leadership to their subordinates. It comprises 14 percent of all undiscussables and 29 percent of issues related to management practice. In effect, the largest single category of undiscussable issues was the boss's interpersonal style.

TABLE 2
Undiscussable Issues

Category	Percentage of Responses
Management practice	49
Co-worker performance	10
Compensation and benefits	6
EEO practices	6
Change	4
Personnel systems (other than pay)	4
Individual feelings	2
Performance feedback to me	2
Bad news	2
Conflicts	2
Personal problems	2
Suggestions for improvement	2
Other	9

Other aspects of management practice which were identified as undiscussable are:

- Decision making—how decisions get made and the quality of decisions
- Favoritism
- The boss's role in promotions, assignments, and terminations
- Information flow that does not relate to decision making
- Too heavy a workload
- Ethics
- Assumptions about management motives
- Corporate politics

"Co-worker performance," at 10 percent, represents the second largest cluster of responses. It includes how well peers do the technical aspects of their jobs, as well as their personal conduct and interaction in the work environment.

"Compensation and benefits" includes concerns about pay equity and benefits as well as the way such systems are administered.

"Equal employment opportunity (EEO) practices" combines any references to affirmative action, equal employment, or related aspects of workplace harassment or discrimination.

"Change" is a small category, but one that primarily reflects the concerns we heard about specific changes which had been implemented in various organizations we visited. People also talked to us about their perception of how much things in general seemed to be changing around them.

"Personnel systems" includes organizational systems other than those that relate to compensation or benefits, such as hiring, promotion, termination or transfer, and employee development.

"Individual feelings" includes the personal emotions people have that relate to their work or work environment.

"Performance feedback to me" reflects a lack of comment—positive or negative—about someone's performance.

"Bad news" refers to negative or critical messages or observations about individuals' or the organization's performance.

"Conflicts" are actual or potential interpersonal disagreements that escalate to a higher level of open conflict.

"Personal problems" includes various types of trouble a person experiences that are not related to work—divorce, illness in the family, financial troubles, drug and alcohol problems, or interpersonal difficulties.

"Suggestions for improvements" consists of ideas or suggestions about doing something differently and better.

"Other" undiscussables were a mixed bag of issues and individual concerns that fit no common pattern.

THEMES AND OBSERVATIONS

During our interviews, we saw many emerging themes in these undiscussed, unresolved workplace issues.

Management Practice Is a Clear Focus for Undiscussables

People find it very difficult to talk to their bosses about management style, actions, or competence. Undiscussables that fell into this category outnumbered any other category at least four to one.

There Was No Basic Difference in Undiscussables from One Level of the Organization to the Next

We sense that factors such as the quality of interaction with a boss, self-confidence, skill level, and experience have a bigger influence on whether a person speaks up than that person's level in the organization.

Items Related to Human Resources Issues and Systems Totaled 16 Percent of Undiscussables

These are the systems and practices that can significantly influence the experience a person has in an organization. How a person is recruited and hired, paid, evaluated, developed, promoted—or fired—says a lot about what the organization believes about people. Perceived inequities, discrimination, or other forms of unfairness in these areas concern people a great deal. Human resources issues surface again in Chapter Six when we report the behaviors that cause people to be afraid.

People Voice Very Carefully Worries About Race, Gender, Age, or Other Harassment or Discrimination

Although virtually all types of discrimination surfaced in our interviews, the most difficult for people to talk about were issues of sexual preference. Discrimination of all kinds warrants continued attention. The educational efforts of the 1980s have obviously not put these issues to rest. Due to the limited scope of this book, we do not directly recommend approaches that deal with these sensitive concerns. They are broad and complex in nature, and the strategies needed to address them require thorough exploration of their cultural and historical background. Our goal in this work is to highlight key points and stimulate a general effort to improve relationships at work. We heartily endorse further work which enables discrimination and harassment issues to surface more easily and be addressed constructively.

Problems with Co-Workers Were Less Frequent Than Those Related to Bosses

This did not surprise us. We anticipate, however, that peer relations and performance will become a more important area of discussion as organizations become flatter in their structures and work is increasingly organized around teams. In our last chapter we briefly suggested ways to build stronger peer teams; we see this as an important step to reducing the amount of fear in an organization.

People Rarely Said That They Were Unable to Speak Up About Necessary Improvements or Innovations

This was a most interesting observation to us. When we started working on this topic, we believed—and still do—that fear of repercussions causes people to remain silent about ideas they have for improvements or innovation. And yet when we asked people to name the topics they hesitated to talk about, only 28 out of 925 responses indicated that people could not talk about a different approach or suggestions for improvement. We believe that the following two factors influence these dynamics:

People will deal with their personal concerns first.   A University of Texas study done in the 1960s helps to explain this pattern by documenting that an individual's reaction will always be personal before it will ever be focused on organizational concerns (Hall, 1979). When people are faced with new, ambiguous, or threatening situations, they have emotional reactions that understandably relate to their self-interest. They wonder, for example,

> 66 *How can I make this situation as successful as possible?* 99

> 66 *What could go wrong here and is there possible harm for me?* 99

> 66 *How can I protect myself from the unknown?* 99

When management performance or organizational systems make life uncomfortable or more complicated, people naturally focus on self-protection and staying out of trouble. They are much less likely to be thinking about the success or failure of business strategies and how their ideas might make a positive contribution. We think that when the need to worry about self-protection diminishes, people will be more interested in offering ideas about organizational improvements.

Employees are culturally programmed not to trust their bosses. One of the reasons why concerns about management show up so often is that they are symbolic of a culture of mistrust and blame. This pattern is embedded deeply in the history and values of this country. Part of our national culture dictates an active mistrust of hierarchy and conformity and an appreciation of competition and rebellion. In the boss-subordinate relationship, a win-lose mentality is combined with suspicion about authority. This may be one of the reasons we are more likely to hear complaints and blame than to see cooperation and trust.

When employees focus on self-interest and see their bosses as the competition, they will not be concerned about making creative contributions to the organization. "Them versus us" thinking does not lead to collaborative problem solving.

ILLUSTRATIONS OF UNDISCUSSABLES

One of the reasons undiscussable issues are so powerful is that they create a self-perpetuating cycle all their own. They create fear and they are the product of fear, all at the same time. Three situations illustrate this dynamic.

Case I: Takeover and Transition

Undiscussables can remain underground for a long time, all the while taking their toll on communication, morale, and organizational effectiveness. Our experiences with a small southeastern manufacturing company that had been bought by a larger corporation demonstrated this unfortunate and expensive pattern. With the new ownership came new people. In fact, the person who had previously been in charge was demoted. Before this change was made, however, the former executive had publicly confronted the incoming CEO about several uncomfortable aspects of the transition. The exchange was heated and public. Once the change in position was implemented, this public disagreement was remembered by almost everyone remaining in the organization.

Even though the public explanation for the change had to do with the superior technical skills of the new person in charge, the public disagreement became the standard explanation for the previous executive losing his position. Because people linked this early confrontation to the demotion, a variety of fear-related patterns were established. First, people decided that they could not speak up to the new owners. After all, there was "proof positive" that repercussions would result from such action. Second, all sorts of related undiscussables resulted:

- How people felt about the new company and many of its technical methods and procedures
- The management style of the new boss
- Office politics regarding a slow-burning power struggle between the old and new bosses
- People throughout the organization taking sides with the "old way" or the "new way"
- Contradictory standards for handling customer complaints

It was not until five years later, when we were asked to consult, that these undiscussables surfaced—along with a tremendous amount of misperception, mistrust, and fear that had built up over time. There is probably no way to estimate the amount of wasted time, energy, and commitment associated with this unfortunate set of circumstances. Conflict had become rampant. People talked about their inability to solve even fairly straightforward problems without getting into arguments. Around and around it went until an outsider asked a few focused questions that brought the background issues to light. Until these issues could be addressed, there was little chance to make use of the employees' skills and strong underlying commitment to their work.

Case II: Never Enough Time to Do It Right

One way in which undiscussables can affect organizational success is clear: If employees hesitate to voice concerns or pass along necessary information, those in charge risk making flawed decisions and unrealistic commitments to customers. Such actions waste resources. Depending on its size, a poorly considered decision or commitment can end up costing considerable money and embarrassing both the organization and key managers. Our second case shows how this can happen.

One manufacturing organization we included in our study places a great deal of emphasis on meeting customers' requirements. This also holds true for the staff departments that provide service to operational field units. The talk about commitment to customers seems dysfunctionally strong. A common question asked of a staff department manager who is making a commitment to deliver a service at a particular time is "Will you stake your job on it?" While this question is typically raised in a joking manner, it nonetheless worries people. They know there is a serious side to the statement.

Predictably, this extreme service commitment mentality is undiscussable. Many believe that in this organization, it is not acceptable to say that a schedule is unworkable. As a consequence, as one manager told us, it is impossible to say "This won't work" until it's too late, "even when they have known about it for a long time." Several times we heard stories about delivery dates being postponed—but not until the eleventh hour. Another person commented: "This really is one of those places where there is never enough time to do it right, but always enough time to do it over. People here won't listen to a lesser level when we ask for more time up front."

The long-term impact of this undiscussable is organizational mismanagement and dissatisfied customers—the very opposite of what was intended. In addition, employees become disillusioned and cynical as a result of a continued pattern of undiscussable service commitments. People do not like working in environments where they cannot voice their concerns. They become frustrated and angry at having to avoid these concerns or hide problems. To many this feels like being asked to lie.

Case III: The Emergency Room Crisis

Our third example, this time involving a hospital emergency room, illustrates how mismanagement and alienated employees could have caused the collapse of an entire operational unit. Once again, undiscussables and an obvious fear of repercussions were at the center of the situation.

The nurse manager for the emergency room (ER) hired a new assistant nurse manager from out of state to run the ER operations. Very quickly, the assistant manager began changing procedures and insisting that her way was the only right way. Upon observing her interaction with patients, the nurses worried that she was providing outdated and—in some cases—unsafe patient care. When the nursing staff would suggest alternatives or try to explain why their current practices worked, she abrasively ignored their advice. This reinforced the belief of many on the nursing staff that her nursing skills were deficient.

After six weeks, the nurse manager brought the nursing staff together because she was concerned that they were not adequately supporting the new assistant. When the staff expressed their concerns about the assistant's dogmatic approach, they were told that if the nurse manager heard of anyone making things hard for the assistant, she would "deal with that person on an individual basis." As a result, the staff nurses decided to "back off and do things our own way as much as we could. Even so, we tried to help [the assistant], but she wouldn't listen. Finally, a group of us couldn't take it any more and started looking for other options."

After six months, one-third of the ER nursing staff, mostly veteran nurses, had found other jobs. Their plan was to leave all at once, to protest what they saw as both incompetent management and poor clinical practice. Two physicians who were equally upset with the tactics of the assistant nurse manager said they also would leave if the nurses left. When she heard what was about to happen, the nurse manager finally began to listen to and believe the staff nurses. She talked with each individually. Within a week, the assistant resigned. Staff nurses were highly involved in the selection of the next assistant manager, and things are now working well.

The actual—as well as the potential—cost of this episode was significant. As one nurse said, "All of our spare time was spent dealing with this situation instead of doing something productive. Many of us used lots of sick time because we just couldn't handle coming to work if she was there."

On a larger scale, the hospital had made a concerted effort in the previous five years to be designated as a regional trauma center. Management, physicians, and the nursing staff had worked hard to streamline their procedures, augment their equipment, and build a solid reputation with medics and firefighters who represented a primary segment of customers. The dynamics of this situation put all this hard work at risk. One staff nurse commented: "This almost destroyed the ER.

I could see why the medics would have gone to other hospitals. Why should they come here to get their heads ripped off by the assistant? She didn't treat anybody with respect. She didn't seem to understand that the medics don't have to bring patients here.''

This nurse found herself apologizing to the paramedics and "then feeling terrible for it. Why should I have had to do that? I'd spend part of my shift smoothing the feathers of other RNs and MDs. I took it on myself because I didn't want to see our reputation being destroyed. I'm very proud of my work and where I work. Yet people were being hurt and I couldn't stand that.''

On the surface, this incident sounds extreme. And yet, from our experience, it is not. What separates it from countless other front-line experiences is that a sizable portion of the key staff were not just thinking about, talking about, or threatening to quit. They had a specific, unified plan that they were ready to put into action.

The nurses were ready to do this because they believed that the nurse manager refused to hear their concerns about the way the assistant manager was running the ER. They also sensed that there would be repercussions for individuals who persisted with their complaints. This only reinforced the staff's perception that the assistant manager's behavior was something they could not talk about. As such, this perception exerted a strong and negative influence on their work and potentially on their careers.

In response to the undiscussable issues, the ER nurses consolidated their opinion that the only way to respond was to retaliate in turn, according to the only real power they perceived themselves to have. By quitting, they would paralyze operations, embarrass the nursing manager, and, they hoped, awaken her to the truth about her assistant's questionable skills.

When we put ourselves in the shoes of the nurse manager, we view a different set of circumstances. We see:

- The nurse manager wanting to support her new assistant's authority in a new job
- Staff nurses who may be stuck in their ways and resistant to new leadership
- Possible uncooperative attitudes and nonsupportive behavior on the part of staff nurses
- An assistant nurse manager who is doing her best in a tough, high-visibility situation

Undiscussable issues were the invisible, unspeakable glue that kept this dangerous cycle in place. Because the staff RNs perceived that their concerns were not welcome, their frustration was driven underground and led to an extreme plan of action. Because the nurse manager thought the staff nurses were being resistant, she did not fully observe and understand the impact of her assistant's management style.

From a long-term perspective, it is lucky that one-third of the nursing staff and two physicians were ready to quit. Had such a dramatic threat to the operation not surfaced, steps might never have been taken to correct the heavy-handed practices of the assistant nurse manager. We can speculate that without this action having been taken, any nurse willing to openly express anger or resentment could easily have been branded as uncooperative and as harmful to the ER leadership. Fortunately, in fact, just the opposite was true. Staff nurses' views and concerns were listened to. Their involvement in the selection of a new assistant manager was an important demonstration of this change.

What people cannot talk about can hurt the organization in a big way. We believe that understanding and identifying undiscussables is the fastest way to figure out what people are afraid of in an organization. Getting rid of undiscussables is a primary step in reducing the presence and impact of fear on organizational success. With an understanding of *what* people are reluctant to talk about, the next step to explore is *why* people do not speak up. Chapter Four is about the answers to that question.

4

THE
REPERCUSSIONS
OF
SPEAKING UP

The individuals we interviewed gave four primary explanations for not speaking up: fear of repercussions, a sense that speaking up would do no good, a desire to avoid conflict, and a reluctance to cause trouble for others. However, fear of repercussions was far and away the reason most frequently cited. In fact, at least 70 percent

---

41

of all the people we interviewed said that one of the reasons they did not speak up in certain situations was because they feared some type of repercussion.

When we asked people why they did not talk about their undiscussable issues, we heard similar patterns and nuances about fear of repercussions whether we were speaking to executives, blue-collar employees, professionals, middle managers, or any other category in our sample. People talked to us about two types of repercussions: first, the delayed, subtle threats frequently connected to ambiguous situations or the ambiguous behavior of their boss, and second, the more immediate, direct repercussions that were usually associated with a manager's abrasive behavior. They told us about an incredible range of anxieties—everything from fear of being cut out of high-level discussions to worries that they would be "reorganized" or harassed out of a job. And they also told us that the starting point for these potential repercussions was often a subtle loss of credibility and reputation. Of all feared repercussions, loss of credibility was the one most frequently cited.

This chapter examines in detail how these anxieties, particularly the subtle ones related to credibility and reputation, powerfully control people's behavior at work. Later in the chapter, we touch on the other reasons people do not speak up and draw possible connections between these reasons and fear.

WHAT PEOPLE ARE AFRAID TO LOSE

When people told us that they did not talk about their undiscussable issues because of fear of some repercussion, we asked the question: What are you afraid will happen? Their answers are summarized in Table 3.

"Loss of credibility or reputation" includes being seen as a troublemaker, boat rocker, agitator, or not a team player, or being given other labels that mark the individual as a problem to the organization; this category also includes fear of losing influence or of being seen as not possessing good judgment or acting in an unprofessional way.

"Loss of career or financial advancement" includes losing one's chances for promotion, being rated down on performance appraisals, and losing pay increases, bonuses, or other discretionary perks.

"Possible damage to relationship with boss" includes antagonizing or upsetting the boss, engaging in a confrontation or criticism which

TABLE 3
Major Fears of Employees

Repercussion	Percentage of Responses
Loss of credibility or reputation	27
Lack of career or financial advancement	16
Possible damage to relationship with boss	13
Loss of employment	11
Interpersonal rejection	9
Change in job role	6
Embarrassment/loss of self-esteem	5
Job transfer or demotion	4
Other	9

could lead to difficulties or long-term tensions, having fears about the boss "making life unlivable at work," and other similar comments.

"Loss of employment" is the fear of being fired, but almost always through a less direct approach, such as being laid off during a downsizing or reorganization, having job tasks pulled away until no assignments are left, or being harassed until one quits.

"Interpersonal rejection" consists of being disliked as a result of speaking up, being seen as not fitting in the organization, not having the right image, or being isolated or shunned by others.

"Change in job role" expresses fears that small changes in assignments will take place, such as no longer being able to participate in certain meetings; that choice assignments will be given to others and less desirable assignments will be given to the employee; or that subtle changes will be made in the role and importance of the employee's work.

"Embarrassment/loss of self-esteem" includes being embarrassed or humiliated in front of others, particularly one's peers or powerful people in the organization, and fear of looking ignorant or unskillful.

"Job transfer or demotion" includes being sent to another part of the company or being given a job with less status or money.

LOSS OF CREDIBILITY AND THE POWER OF LABELS

The loss of credibility and reputation is most commonly expressed as a fear of being labeled. Words like "troublemaker," "boat rocker," and "unprofessional" worry people. They convey poor judgment, last a long time, and lead to other, more tangible repercussions. These words imply that an individual is acting in bad faith and operating against the interests of the organization. They connote being an outsider. Many see that being labeled "not a team player" is the beginning of a downward cycle where duties start to change and performance ratings decline. These events, in turn, influence career opportunities, raises, and bonuses, and can possibly lead to layoffs or transfers. In many organizations, the concept of the "hit list" represents the extreme outcome of fears about being labeled.

Labels are signals of disfavor that quietly operate in the minds of managers and supervisors. People often believe that over time these psychological sorting bins control the ultimate success or failure of people in the organization. Once a loss of credibility has occurred, other incremental repercussions begin to accumulate. The person may be cut out of an important information loop, lose a key tie to decision makers, or lose the respect of those the individual most admires. The individual may no longer be seen as an important contributor. The ultimate message is, "You may be good enough to stay, but don't expect to be recognized or important, to have influence, or to get the support you want."

Loss of credibility and reputation is defined as being much larger than a question of performance. It is experienced in the broad realm of ego and self-esteem, not just the local geography of tasks and specific skills. A vice-president of a service firm defined credibility as "your boss's trust in your judgment." Other members of our sample described it as "people's faith in you," "trust of your motives," and "your validity as a person." These definitions are about core integrity as a human being. Labeling, they are saying, is felt as an attack on the person, not just on the performer. As one thirty-year veteran of a large corporation put it, "When your judgment is in question, it is very, very serious. Judgment is *everything*."

What makes the issue of credibility so complex, controlling, and frightening for people is that the labels are usually believed to be hidden. Many are convinced that management's subtle, derogatory conclusions about someone's credibility translate into negative consequences. But they also believe that the connection between the two will be obscured by time and false explanations. They will be dimmed by decision makers' own lack of awareness that they are using them to make critical choices. Hence the concern to avoid, as a bank employee told us, any "slight, negative background feeling." Better to stick with the party line. Better not to rock the boat by speaking up.

People fear that a loss of credibility is final, silent, and permanent. One small group of interviewees repeatedly referred to "the memory bank of the organization." Another talked about "the area under the curve," meaning management's accounting of a person's total reputation and accomplishments, which includes both positive and negative events. The consensus in that group was that "one 'aw shit' wiped out all previous achievements under the curve. Another interviewee observed: "When your career is hurt because your credibility has been questioned, you're never involved in the discussion and you'll never be able to prove it."

CHARACTERISTICS OF SUBTLE, INDIRECT REPERCUSSIONS

Over half of the stories we heard about repercussions were about the indirect, subtle consequences associated with speaking up. These stories were characterized by four themes:

Subtle Repercussions Have Large Potential Impact

66 *I was asked to put together some figures and make a presentation to a senior manager of the company. The figures were not favorable to the company, but they were true. When I presented them, my VP and boss didn't support me. My boss said, 'Yes, Margaret, you had better redo those numbers.' I was never again invited to a senior management meeting.* **99**

—**Program analyst**

66 *I've seen the way they push people out. Take work away from people little by little. Transfer responsibilities to others. Everybody smiles, but the job is very small.* **99**

—**First-line supervisor**

Subtle Repercussions Are Untraceable

A fourth-level manager for a major corporation, demoted many months after he criticized a marketing program, speaks of the vice-president he offended:

> 66 He never came to me. He carried out the demotion in the
> classic large organization way, by assassinating reputations and
> careers without me knowing where it came from. 'Why are you
> moving the job to Omaha?' I asked my boss. He said, 'That's
> just the way we are going to do it.' 99

Subtle Repercussions Are Unpredictable

> 66 People are not afraid of what will happen to them tomorrow.
> They worry about what will happen down the road in six months
> or so. 99
>
> —**Technical worker**

A senior deputy of a government agency, voicing similar concerns about his boss's reaction to certain topics, said:

> 66 It will come back on other issues—unpredictably,
> unrecognizably. 99

Subtle Repercussions Are Not Contestable

A professional-level employee worries about how salary decisions are being made behind closed doors. He is anxious about how managers discuss individuals' performance together, "when the anecdotes and labels come up."

A corporation attorney indicates:

> 66 I'm where I want to be now. Will they force me to transfer
> back to headquarters? There is the danger that if there is a
> downsizing, you want to be close enough to old Jack so that he
> doesn't send you back there. It's not even a conscious thing. 99

These four characteristics are a central part of why people do not speak up. They express the qualities that create a sense of danger and helplessness. As one person in our sample said, they generate a low-key, "long-enduring mental anxiety." The characteristics especially highlight the importance of maintaining a polished reputation and a good relationship with the boss.

THE ABRASIVE BOSS AND IMMEDIATE, DIRECT REPERCUSSIONS

Damage to one's relationship with the boss represents a powerful cross-current to the indirect repercussions just identified. It is further testament to how significantly people see relationships with their supervisors. Subtle repercussions are not the only kind. People also see their supervisors as potential sources of immediate discomfort and pain. They particularly fear being trapped in a stressful relationship, working for someone who insults them and is abrasive, critical, and autocratic.

The possibility of working for an abrasive boss plays a special role in the dynamic of people's fears. Unlike the characteristics of indirect repercussions, those that come from an abrasive or abusive supervisor may be anything but subtle, disconnected, unpredictable, or based on hidden assumptions.

This means that at the same time people are concerned about what is happening behind the scenes, they may also have to deal with a different kind of fear about their work environment. For example, a person might worry about an indirect repercussion such as being kept out of certain meetings and decisions or having contact blocked with important associates in other divisions. If this person reports to a boss with abrasive or abusive tendencies, she may have to worry about much more: her work being constantly scrutinized; unpredictable requests or demands for overtime work; public embarrassment and criticism; and sarcastic innuendo or direct verbal assaults on her character, competence, or credibility.

When these two types of fear combine they play off one another in an extremely volatile way, creating an experience of enormous stress. A highly experienced clerical employee told this story about her job with a manufacturing firm:

> 66 I got a new boss. She didn't want anybody in the department who had worked there longer than her. She was very insecure. She wanted everybody to learn her way. She would choose a particular part of the department for critiquing. From then on, nothing good could come out of that area. People who had been there for years were suddenly inept, and were let go. They were always let go on Friday night. This happened four times. Then I knew it was my turn.

" She was a barracuda. I went over her head to protect my job. I worked there for two more years. It was misery. Every day was like walking on dynamite. My productivity went down because I was watching every word. I called it 'ulcer gulch.' There was constant dread, and in fact I developed ulcers.

" I went to the CEO. He said he couldn't perceive this person doing these things. They take the attitude that if you complain it must be a vendetta. I think he dismissed it as a woman-versus-woman conflict.

" It was a nightmare. She criticized people openly. Made obscene comments to a co-worker. Humiliated people. I thought about the situation twenty-four hours a day, playing over the incidents that might happen. In some cases these things actually did happen.

" I stayed because of pride. I knew I was right. It would have been an admission of defeat if I had quit. It was a question of self-esteem. I took the attitude: 'You can't make me go away feeling like I didn't do a good job.' "

While such situations are rare, we did hear a number of similar stories. Most people do not run across the "ogre boss" in their careers, but there are enough abrasive supervisors and managers to keep the threat of their presence abundant. We are convinced that stories about abrasive supervisors spread far and wide within organizations, even if the relative number of such people is small. Insofar as companies tolerate their abrasive behavior, they risk strengthening the fear that repercussions—subtle or otherwise—are a way of life at work. This tolerance also sends a message to employees that the organization condones or even supports this style of management.

OTHER REPERCUSSIONS

As we have already pointed out, we see loss of credibility as the starting point for other, more concrete losses such as those involving career and money, employment loss, change in job role, and job transfer or demotion. Table 3 highlighted the variety of repercussions people are worried about. In some organizations, transfer seemed to be the preferred method for dealing with those who had lost their credibility. In one corporation comments included the phrase, "No one ever gets fired—just sent away on the inside." In this organization, people also worried about their job responsibilities being changed, in effect, creating a "nothing job." In another organization, we were told that the CEO openly bragged during a management training session about how many top people he had sent off to some organizational Siberia over the years.

Interpersonal rejection and embarrassment or loss of self-esteem, like loss of credibility, are intangible repercussions that may have significant and concrete long-term effects. Interpersonal rejection emphasizes the degree to which people believe they will be pushed out of the organization because they do not "fit" its image. They must win approval as being the right "type." Interpersonal rejection means being ostracized, and as one interview participant expressed it, "Very few people come back from being shunned."

We visited one organization with a flat structure and high levels of employee participation. As a result, peer relationships surfaced as being of great importance. Correspondingly, interpersonal rejection from co-workers emerged as a significant fear. People worried that they would not be seen as fitting "The XYZ Company Way."

Embarrassment and loss of self-esteem reflect the power individuals' self-images have over their conduct. Fear of "looking like an idiot" is a self-inflicted repercussion that can be triggered by a sense of rejection from others or by a damaged reputation. This fear can be a sizable barrier for self-critical people who want to see themselves as consistently competent, knowledgeable, and sensitive. In the long term it undermines contributions and may therefore have an indirect impact on achievements, opportunities, and careers.

How Real Are the Repercussions?

This list of repercussions may raise the question of how realistic these fears are. Do these repercussions really occur? When time permitted in our interviews, we asked people to tell us more about the way in which they became afraid. Were there actual events they could point to where obvious repercussions had taken place? Or was there some other dynamic at work? These discussions helped us to understand the continuum in Figure 1.

We are convinced that many people have actual experiences in which they suffered repercussions from speaking up. The most obvious situations involve abrasive or abusive bosses who are usually well known for extracting some type of payment from people who challenge their way of doing things. We have come to believe,

Actual repercussions	Perceived repercussions	Imagined repercussions

Figure 1. Experiences with Repercussions

however, that the percentage of actual repercussions is far less than those which are perceived or imagined.

Perceived repercussions are those where people believe they have been harmed and there is a plausible, but not certain, connection to management behavior. *Imagined repercussions* are identical, except that the connection to management behavior is tenuous. In organizations where bosses—at whatever level—are mistrusted and viewed with suspicion, a small number of actual repercussions is usually magnified many times. This sets in motion a pattern that causes people to perceive threat when none is intended. It encourages others to imagine all sorts of horrible things that "might happen" because "you never know what the boss might decide to do." The mix of reality and unexplained or ambiguous situations sets in motion a wave of perceptions that contain both truth and possibility.

As we have said before, fear is not a rational topic. People's fears are real, if not all their facts. It does not matter if the perception or imagination is grounded in "reality." The issue is the fact that individuals hesitate to speak up because they fear some type of harm if they do. A senior-level engineer told us that he worries about possible repercussions. When we asked if there had been actual cases of repercussions, he immediately answered, "Oh, yes." When we asked for details he vividly recalled an event that had taken place *eight years* earlier.

We know that people believe very strongly in the *possibility* of repercussions. This is often the case even when they cannot name a specific situation or tell a distinct story verifying that repercussions have occurred. As one person neatly summarized:

> **❝** If you get to the point where you should speak up, you look at how your boss has treated you over the past few months. Were you put down in front of co-workers? Was your pride or dignity insulted? Did the choice assignments go someplace else? **❞**

If the answer to these questions is yes, *or if people believe the answer could be yes,* the response is usually the same: silence.

THE OTHER REASONS FOR NOT SPEAKING UP

As mentioned at the beginning of this chapter, there were four primary reasons why people do not talk about their undiscussable issues. We have chosen to concentrate on the fear of repercussions because it is such a strong and central theme. Table 4 provides a breakdown of how people responded to questions about why they do not speak up.

When we asked people about their reasons for staying silent on issues of concern, we collected 415 different responses. Forty-four percent of these answers involved anxiety about repercussions. While most people gave a variety of general responses, seven out of ten people specifically mentioned repercussions as at least one of their reasons. When these two figures are considered together, they create a compelling documentation of fear in the workplace.

Next in importance to fear of repercussions, "Nothing will change" responses stood out. These responses were often characterized by a sense of cynicism or futility, a feeling of certainty that speaking up would come to nothing.

66 *I'm a peon; management is powerful.* 99

—**Internal auditor**

66 *Management turns its back.* 99

—**Lead assembler**

66 *My boss says, 'Uh huh, uh huh,' but doesn't do anything about the problem.* 99

—**Clerical employee**

TABLE 4
Why People Do Not Speak Up

Reason	Percentage of Responses
Fear of repercussions	44
Nothing will change	17
Avoidance of conflict	7
Don't want to cause trouble for others	5
Miscellaneous	27

These comments all reflect the belief that options have been cut off and there is simply no point in trying anything further. One accounting professional, for example, talked about his belief that his manager simply "doesn't value input" and gives the impression that "he's better than you are." The employee felt "helpless, stymied." This sort of experience can lead to the firm conclusion that speaking up is a waste of time. As another employee, also convinced that he had nothing to gain, put it, "Why bust my pick?"

Without systematically assessing these responses, we found that they seemed to divide themselves into two groups: first, employees who had tried to speak up and had gotten nowhere, and second, employees who had not tried very hard to open an issue but who nevertheless were convinced that nothing would come of it if they did. These responses are like other aspects of mistrust. They are muddied by negative expectations and interpretations. We are convinced that like fear of repercussions, powerlessness is real and is also expanded by perceptions, feelings, and past experiences.

We do not claim to understand the exact relationship between fear and powerlessness, although a number of potential connections do exist. A middle manager reported to us how long battles with the fear of repercussions from a new boss eventually led to a long-term sense of frustration. "Now," she says, "it is more that I feel speaking up is hopeless." Another person made it clear that she feels it is easier to feel powerless than fearful. "I won't allow myself to even consider the fear." Another suggested that she never even gets to a point of worry about repercussions since she seldom speaks out, because she is so convinced it will do no good.

Whatever the connection, it is apparent that the sense of powerlessness is as debilitating as fear itself. It forces people to live with organizational realities they want to see improved, realities which keep them from being fully productive or satisfied about their jobs. Our experience as consultants has taught us that a sense of powerlessness often leads to cynicism and complaints. This convinces managers that employees are either "whining" or just plain resistant to change. Managers wonder why efforts to "empower" their people seem to take so long. We would suggest that in addition to the powerlessness, fear is also taking its toll, and until the fear is dealt with constructively, techniques to grant authority to employees may well be treated with suspicion.

The categories "Avoidance of conflict" and "Don't want to cause trouble for others" both reflect an interest in maintaining harmony and are flip sides of the same coin. Some people do not wish to bring up sensitive issues in order to prevent themselves or others from getting hurt. Like the fear of repercussions and powerlessness, these two responses also stabilize and control behavior. This is consistent with Argyris's (1986) perspective on defensive behaviors, which states that they maintain the status quo. At bottom such responses probably reflect a fear of disturbing relationships which might be difficult to restore. For those who are not confident of their ability to manage conflict, the fear of participating in an open argument would be as much a barrier to speaking up as any type of repercussion.

Last, the "Miscellaneous" category reflects a wide array of other explanations and personal interpretations. It includes such responses as:

66 *It would cause an awkward conversation.* 99

66 *It would violate my sense of propriety about who should take the message forward.* 99

66 *Maybe it's only a personal perception of the problem.* 99

People also reported that they do not speak up because they do not see it as part of their role or job, that they lack the confidence to "even know what to say," and that they do not want to get involved or expose how they really feel about an issue.

The fear expressed to us in our interviews, along with the other causes of not speaking up, represent invisible, rarely discussed barriers to participation and contribution. They make the grade steeper and the way less clear. These fears sap the energy people need to fulfill high standards for performance. As we explore in the next chapter, this impact can be enormous.

5

THE
HIGH COST
OF FEAR

O ne manager we interviewed explained that topics like fear are not talked about at higher levels in his organization because executives have a low tolerance for ambiguity. "Either it burns more fuel or less—they want to know the right answer," he told us. Unfortunately, he was entirely right about assessing the intangible qualities and influence of fear. Measuring its impact is neither easy nor exact.

Fear's cost largely comes down to figuring the influence of negative emotions on people's work. As we interviewed, we asked individuals to identify how fear affected their feelings, relationships, quality of work, and productivity. While their answers were highly negative, they—and we—found it very difficult to translate the responses into concrete costs. It was like trying to calculate the dollar impact of a dissatisfied customer.

The responses of those we interviewed, however, do provide a broad and provocative picture of the intangible costs of fear. This is a picture of a "silent organization" made up of people who do not speak up about their concerns or their ideas for improvements and innovations. Responses to our questions about the impact of fear reveal what it is like to be part of the silent organization. In Table 5 we report this impact; we then illustrate important themes with the individual experiences of those we interviewed.

Negative Feelings About the Organization

Included in this area are loss of trust or pride, increase in political or self-protective behavior, contemplated or real job transfers, and petty revenge or sabotage.

Loss of Trust or Pride

The largest set of responses had to do with a loss of trust or pride in the organization. People said that they became less dedicated or committed. As one long-term, very loyal employee of a bank stated, "I need to be proud of where I work." Undiscussables and fear of repercussions undermine the ability to experience this pride.

Speaking of an undiscussable change in business philosophy, a staff member of the same organization stated:

> 66 The bank has changed its relationship to its employees. Loyalty, trust, and the family sense are gone. It's them and us—they would lay you off tomorrow if it fit a corporate interest. This certainly has reduced loyalty in return. I wouldn't recommend this bank to a friend. 99

TABLE 5
The Impact of Fear

Issue	Percentage of Responses
Negative feelings about the organization	29
Negative impact on quality or productivity	27
Negative feelings about oneself	19
Negative emotions	12
Other negative effects	11
Positive effects	2

Another person in the same organization commented:

> 66 *There isn't a free give and take on the job. It didn't use to be that way—it used to be more people oriented. Competition is now so great, they've forgotten that people are here. Feelings don't matter. We've gotten younger men [as senior managers] and competition between these men is great. We are made to feel that we should be as competitive as they are. It makes us mad and scares us. Each shift in management gets a little worse.* 99

Increase in Political or Self-Protective Behavior

Others, adapting to their loss of faith in the company, look for alternative routes to success or survival. A senior manager described this process in terms of people learning that "connections" are what is important. The end result, he said, was the creation of "Teflon™ people," to whom nothing can stick. A supervisor told us:

> 66 *I really want to approach people on a face-value basis, but around here politics are everywhere. Some people just have the right connections. Merit doesn't have much to do with it, so I'm looking for a mentor to help me get ahead. I know that the people who get ahead are liked by senior management. If you smile the right way you can get the job.* 99

Another aspect of self-protective behavior is the time spent engaging in "CYA" activities. For example, a number of individuals commented that they kept note files on what was happening to them or around them or in their work. "I document to cover my ass," an experienced social services worker told us. He was afraid of being audited because "I may not be able to sustain it. Because we are overloaded, they can always find something wrong. People have been targeted and lost their jobs."

In another interview, a mid-level manager pulled a list from his drawer of thirty-four company officers fired during the previous eight years. He assured us that this did not include people who had left the organization of their own volition. His reason for keeping the list was so that if he was fired he could negotiate an equitable separation package based on what other terminated managers had received. He also commented how in past times in his organization, people had been so fearful of being blamed for problems or mistakes that "200 percent of our time was spent documenting decisions. I kept logs of all decisions I made, kept notes at all meetings. Minutes of meetings were signed and dated."

Contemplated or Real Job Transfers

In a number of cases, people told us that as the result of undiscussable issues they thought increasingly about leaving the company or transferring out of the work unit. In one case we were told by a front-line employee that he was confidentially looking for a position outside the organization as a "safety net" in case things went wrong. Much more frequently we heard about situations in which people left their jobs out of disillusionment and frustration. As one senior manager put it, "Why should I be loyal to them if they are not loyal to me?"

We heard many stories where the outcome was a decision to leave due to an abrasive, insensitive, or abrupt boss. One supervisor, for example, reported that she took a sensitive employee relations problem to her boss and got the response, "I have no compassion." The supervisor had already seen the manager treat customers poorly. Later, the manager required her to hire someone she felt was not qualified for the job. These issues, along with other aspects of the manager's controlling style, were all undiscussable. The supervisor therefore initiated an internal transfer. She felt that she had not been treated with respect, and she did not want "her life made miserable" by a boss who would treat her as a "second-class citizen" or only tell her negative things about her performance.

Petty Revenge or Sabotage

Occasionally we would also hear comments about petty revenge or sabotage. For example, one twenty-year employee commented that she would let her boss "stew and sweat" over issues which had become undiscussable. "I become less communicative—the thing he likes the least," she said. "I won't jump in and pick up the pieces. I take the attitude, 'I'm not going to help you out.'"

In another case, a senior vice-president for a financial institution told us that he had pulled his personal retirement accounts and placed them with a competitor after the company's chief financial officer insulted him in front of the chairman.

These responses indicate how people withdraw their support and distance themselves from the organization. They show the effects of a widening gap between the perceived interests of the organization and the interests of the individual. When people feel insulted and afraid they withdraw their allegiance to the company and the boss. We are reminded of a manager in our acquaintance who was once fond of saying, "I expect everything but loyalty. I *demand* loyalty." However, this is just the reverse of what we found to be possible. Loyalty is perhaps the one thing which cannot be demanded.

NEGATIVE IMPACT ON QUALITY OR PRODUCTIVITY

This area includes lack of any extra effort; making and hiding mistakes; failure to meet deadlines and budgets; loss of effective problem solving; work on wrong priorities; poor methods; and loss of creativity, motivation, and risk taking.

Lack of Any Extra Effort

An important pattern emerged for us as we asked people about the impact of fear on productivity. Many people described doing what they were told, but as a result of fear, they did not go beyond expectations or work to their full potential. They came up to the line of a particular performance standard but did not surpass it. In its simplest form, this pattern was often expressed as resentment. A blue-collar store clerk who worked for a critical, manipulative boss related that she had said to a co-worker, "You want thirty rivets? Count them yourself."

The resentment can be lasting and deep. In one situation, for example, an employee had received positive performance appraisals for years but was not promoted in favor of a junior colleague. The reasons for this were unclear to him and, he felt, undiscussable. As a consequence, he began to suspect that there was an unknown, undiscussable "hidden totem" for promotions:

> 66 I asked myself, why would I do extra work? Why would I come in on Saturday? Why not play golf? I felt relegated to a job with the attitude of management that 'it's good enough for you.' I felt very expendable despite the fact that I'd received good feedback about my performance. I decided all I needed to do from then on was eight hours a day. I lost initiative. From then on I let time take care of problems, rather than addressing them directly. I felt hurt. I discounted what the boss said. 99

A manager in another organization told us that he had attempted to talk about some sensitive product cost issues and was cut short by his boss. As a result of this occurrence, he reported:

> 66 I lost interest in doing the things I knew I was supposed to do, like pushing my group to do a better job and lower costs. 'Why bother?' was my watchword. Nobody else cared, so why should I? Why not take the easy way out? It was easy to just let things flow. I found myself getting more tentative with people. I didn't communicate much. I stayed in my office more. Relationships were restrained, unsatisfying. This lasted about six months. 99

People were explicit that where fear and resentment are present, doing extra work only comes from a sense of personal pride, not pride in the company. A social services professional made this point by saying:

> 66 I am going to meet my quota for client placements—past that, what more incentive is there? I do things above and beyond sometimes due to dedication to the program. But I only work forty hours a week. I go above and beyond, but not as far as I could go. 99

Additionally, we heard many comments suggestive of demoralization or burnout:

66 *I didn't give a damn any more.* 99

66 *It's not worth an ulcer. I no longer strive for excellence.* 99

66 *I had a long-term attitude of not caring—I just did the basics to survive in the job.* 99

This point is illustrated well by a meeting between a manager and a group of "survivor" employees after a series of layoffs. The employees had expected to talk about and resolve workload problems in the aftermath of the reduction in force. However, the meeting went poorly and exacerbated the employees' plight:

66 *The executive just talked. She apparently didn't feel comfortable asking for help or decisions from the group. The atmosphere was strained. It came down to saying that things were bad and they were liable to get worse. People didn't really say what was on their minds. It was self-protective. We felt she had the power of life and death. We didn't know her well enough to divulge our feelings. There were no positive strokes or encouragement.*

66 *People talked about this meeting. It didn't advance positive feelings. Perhaps they wouldn't try as hard as a result of it. There was no support. They felt patronized. They thought it was a waste of time.*

66 *We described the problems, but it came down to the executive's attitude that 'we're going to run a tight ship—we can't do everything for everybody.' Most people want to do a good job, but we were left to feel that you couldn't do a good job. It led to some people saying to hell with it or feeling they ought to just walk away. You heard employees saying, 'Maybe they don't want us, they don't care if we leave.'* 99

Making and Hiding Mistakes; Failure to Meet Deadlines and Budgets

In other cases, stressful relationships caused people to make errors in their work or be unable to finish it on time. Several people told us stories about getting caught between supervisors and managers who did not get along. One secretary described a situation where she worked for three managers who were "caught in a three-way spitting contest." She said her efficiency went down, along with her health. "I would check my letters six times. I made stupid mistakes. They get you scared, but they make you inefficient."

A lab worker in a hospital believed that his supervisor was trying to get him fired. The stress of the situation

> **“** clearly impacted the quality of my work. I repeated tests because I was fearful of making mistakes and I knew it would be used against me. I was very tired because of all my shift changes and I know I didn't perform as well as usual. **”**

A quality assurance inspector talked about "mentally double tracking." He said that his concentration was off, forcing him to reinspect his work more frequently.

Not only can people make more mistakes, but they spend time hiding them as well. One of our interviewees recalled problems with broken semiconductors in an assembly operation. The company took what was perceived to be a punitive approach to reducing the number of broken components. The result was more broken parts, but fewer found. People focused on avoiding the punishment, and the stress actually had caused the problem to increase. This experience corresponds exactly to W. Edwards Deming's message about fear—that it prevents management from hearing and seeing the truth (1986, pp. 59–60).

In another company we heard about people routinely adding 20 to 30 percent to "official" estimates of project costs and schedules. People had learned that being realistic would get them in trouble. As a consequence many projects were over cost and schedule, and pressure was high. A manager at this company reported that one of his bosses had a demanding, abrasive personality and would use "verbal slaps in the face" and vulgar language to embarrass and intimidate people. He felt that this boss had been "kept around to get us out of trouble when we were three months behind schedule and had to deliver in three weeks. Veteran managers up the system looked the other way."

We are inclined to believe that there was a connection between the false time and cost estimates and the presence of this abrasive boss. We also sense that any short-term gains this boss might have been responsible for were more than offset by serious morale problems and energy spent by subordinates complaining to the human resources department about his style. After one and a half years of concerted efforts by several managers, the abrasive boss finally was moved to "individual contributor" status. We doubt that this hidden cost ever surfaced on paper.

Loss of Effective Problem Solving; Work on Wrong Priorities; Poor Methods

Another loss in productivity and quality can come from dysfunctional problem-solving efforts, themes highlighted previously in the work of Zand (1972) and Argyris (1986). A deputy director of a large county agency told us:

66 *At weekly management meetings, at least two or three times, there would be an in-depth discussion of a major issue. A manager would be in the midst of it when Stan [the new agency head] would make a terse comment, gather his papers, and leave. People got a confusing message about where and how to bring up significant issues. Now we only talk about peripheral issues. People don't know what to expect from Stan. We are now trying to deal with our need to participate, not just sit there and grunt.* 99

Our interviewees reported that the wrong work was being performed because of their inability to talk through the issue with the boss. In one comparatively small instance, a senior manager calculated that he had spent 80 hours of his own time, plus 145 hours of time from other top staff, to resolve an issue that should have been handled by managers farther down the organization. However, he did this because of potential repercussions from the top executive.

In another case, not just *what* work was done, but *how* the work was accomplished was an undiscussable cost to the organization. A top official talked about an interlocking directorate between a legal firm and his corporation. Most of the corporation's legal work went to that firm. In the official's view, this pattern had permitted corporation managers who did not want to make sensitive or tough decisions to dump them on the law firm. They found a way to get "off the hook" even when the decisions were more operational than legal. And excess legal fees became the norm.

Loss of Creativity, Motivation, and Risk Taking

Other comments illustrated a loss of creative or innovative work and risk taking. The head of another corporate legal office told us that "when someone tries to use fear to motivate me, I get all tied up. I get less creative and less willing take chances, and you've got to take risks to do good work."

Frequently, the "play it safe" mentality becomes deeply ingrained in the culture of the organization. A middle manager with twenty years in his sales and marketing organization commented on *penalties* for creativity: "This company has a long history of introducing change, sometimes not very well. However, those who introduce new ways eventually go away; those who play it safe are the ones who last." A manager supporting European sales in another company echoed a similar thought: "When you get zapped for doing anything wrong, you learn to only do the basics." Or as one person from a telecommunications firm in the Southeast observed, "Nobody gets in trouble if they are not doing anything."

Several managers we spoke with observed that in spite of their organization's talk about innovation and change, no reward systems were in place for people who do take risks. One of them also told the following story about an incident that showed how efforts to increase creativity had been directly shut down by upper management:

66 *An employee task force reported that the company was not fostering creativity. The environment of the meeting immediately became hostile. The VPs became defensive and began citing examples of when ideas had been supported. One of the examples was the brilliant work of an employee which, in fact, had been very hard to gain budget approval for. It was ironic that the VPs would use this as support for their arguments.* 99

The absence of rewards can happen on a small scale but leave a big message with people. A front-line employee had worked hard on a suggestion for developing a form to deal with a discrepant materials problem. She believed that the new document would have saved the company over 80 percent of the cost of the current method for dealing with the problem. However, the suggestion "got lost" and she was reticent to continue asking her supervisor what had happened to it. As an immediate result, the company lost the innovation and her boss lost respect. More importantly, the employee decided that such work was not "worth the risk." To her, the message was clear: Innovation is not part of the job.

A mid-level manager for a West Coast service firm summed up these effects nicely:

66 *Where there is a lot of fear of screwing up, people don't change behaviors or work systems. Creativity is inhibited. People work one day at a time, rather than looking to the future. High fear environments just create 'knee jerking.' You spend all your time putting out fires.* 99

NEGATIVE FEELINGS ABOUT ONESELF

Along with the foregoing effects, individuals also often reported a mild to serious loss of self-esteem. Comments such as the following were common:

66 *Your value as a person is definitely in question.* 99

66 *I was a total mess.* 99

66 *I had a feeling of stress, self-doubts, a trapped feeling.* 99

66 *I take it out on those I can affect—the 'kick the dog' syndrome.* 99

Individuals sometimes criticized themselves unmercifully. In turn, this influenced co-worker and family relationships. A tone of self-criticism is evident in this story from a division manager:

66 *There was criticism from customers. Backlogs. Other divisions felt very frustrated about our performance. We were on the verge of breaking up—totally reorganizing the unit. I felt I should be hesitant to talk to my boss about this. I should be able to handle it. I wanted to be competent. I didn't want to fail. I felt my boss would side against me if I talked to him about it. I was afraid of what his reaction might be. I spent one whole day cleaning out my office. There were a lot of sleepless nights. I made requests for extra people, but he sat on them. I was angry at the other divisions for not supporting me. I was pounding on my people to improve. Finally, I had to let him know we were in trouble.* 99

For most, loss of self-esteem may not be as crippling as in this example, but it definitely undermines performance. When people do not feel good about themselves, they move toward a state of ongoing negativity about their work and their workplace. They operate with greater dependency on the organization and like it less. We believe that this is exactly the opposite of what most people want.

NEGATIVE EMOTIONS AND OTHER NEGATIVE EFFECTS

Even if there is no visible decline in commitment, productivity, or self-esteem, people often experience an array of very negative emotions.

Working through these feelings takes time and energy that could be better spent. A health care professional felt intimidated by her boss and unable to work out a conflict about how she should research a presentation. She reported:

> 66 I didn't do the research I felt I needed to do. I wasn't as prepared as I should have been. I was internally angry, but externally I acquiesced. I felt impotent and inadequate. I had a feeling of distance from others. I was frustrated and confused and felt very unsupported. I commiserated with a lot of other people. 99

Typical emotions people expressed were anger, frustration, depression, disappointment, disillusionment, and tension. "It was like tears choking me inside," a parking attendant told us. "If they didn't want me to work there, they should just say so." As a result of these emotions, and as evidence of their energy-sapping qualities, people sometimes also reported physical effects such as sleeplessness, fatigue, crying, illness, and weight or blood pressure problems. Many people reported time off task at work as they talked about or thought about negative events. They mentally rehearsed how they might handle the future and played back their memories of what had already occurred.

Among this range of emotions, perhaps one of the most devastating, in terms of its impact on people and organizations, is cynicism. Cynicism causes people to assume that the negative feelings are a permanent fixture of the workplace. It is taken for granted that things will not get much better. These feelings serve as a barricade to trying harder, taking risks, and achieving aspirations. A clerical worker told us more about the problem.

> 66 People don't feel safe here. I feel safe but that's because I don't have ambitions. I'm single, no family. I don't have commitments. I have options and I know where I stand. I know enough not to trust this place. What they tell me today is what they are telling me today. They may say something else tomorrow. I feel safe because my eyes are open. 99

In another organization, an employee at about the same level similarly commented, "I know that I'm here because I've learned to play the game. It doesn't matter whether you are good or bad."

There were many other miscellaneous negative effects. For example, some people talked about lawsuits against the company, contemplated or real. One individual recounted a story of how a union was brought in to protect employees even though the initiators of this action did not personally want one. Others identified less dramatic but still significant effects: an information flow that did not follow the chain of command, caution in choosing the people one socialized with outside of work, and a loss of commitment to change efforts within the organization.

POSITIVE EFFECTS

A very small proportion of the responses were of a positive nature. A few people thought that fear-oriented environments caused them to "work their tails off." One professional-level employee felt that fear of competition among peers "kept people sharp" and that the costs "didn't outweigh the benefits." Another professional thought that "paranoia is positive because it causes people to think."

Most responses in this category, however, were coupled with a reservation or two:

> **66** I wouldn't call it a growth experience, but it did force me to cope. **99**

> **66** I have grown a lot. It would be nice to think you shouldn't have to go through this in order for that to happen. **99**

> **66** I am working on not letting fear motivate me. **99**

> **66** Quality improved—what I had control over. I withdrew from the group, was labeled as 'surly, not a team player.' I lost respect for co-workers. I felt helpless and hopeless. There were blowups at home and on the job. I escaped into my work. **99**

CAN FEAR BE A POSITIVE MOTIVATOR?

In about half our interviews we asked people if they thought fear could ever be a positive motivator for people. Over half of the responses were a resounding, "No way!" Fear was considered a *de*-motivator of the worst kind. Many people simply did not respect its use as an effective management approach. Typical comments included the following:

f *People who think they have to frighten someone must have a personality problem or low self-esteem—if fear is the only tool they have to feel more powerful and produce results.* 

f *Those who manage by fear are weak, not confident enough to be open.* 

f *Fear is one of the most despicable methods. There are many other ways to approach people. I generally think it is used indiscriminately and I don't like that. I'm realistic enough to know that it is used, yet naive enough to hope it isn't. In the long run, it's much more productive to use other means. Why use something that doesn't work the best?* 

f *There are better ways to motivate people. Good bosses can do it.* 

f *Fear can get you to stop doing something counterproductive, but it cannot motivate you to do your best.* 

The remaining responses indicated that fear did have some place as a motivator, but only under restricted conditions. Slightly over 10 percent of the responses suggested that fear can be a positive stimulus, but *only* if it is self-imposed. That is, when a person takes on a risk as a personal or professional stretch, fear may be a successful *self-*motivator. Another group of responses reflected the idea that fear could work in the short term but not the long term. And even here there were deficits. As one manager said: "Fear is a constructive motivator only in rare circumstances, and then you pay the price of people resenting you forever." The remaining responses characterized fear as a helpful but limited goad. A handful of people said that at some point, their fear of repercussions had been good for them. Those experiences helped them to get a grip on some of the details of their jobs, develop self-discipline, or put work in perspective with the rest of their lives. However, the overall pattern unequivocally was the belief that externally imposed fear is a negative force with destructive long-term consequences.

THE CUMULATIVE IMPACT OF FEAR

Once the experiences of those in the silent organization are evaluated carefully, the costs are disturbing. The lost commitment, motivation, and confidence, unmeasurable as they may be, can represent an enormous waste of human resources.

One story, in particular, dramatically illustrates how fear not only wastes people but can have a direct impact on the business success of an organization. The story involves a small midwestern company that describes itself as a "Cadillac provider" of mainframe software. The previous CEO was a man frequently described as a "tyrant" by those we interviewed. People at all levels said he created a pervasive climate of fear, a climate so strong that it resulted in the release of a faulty software package originally intended to be the "jewel in the crown" of the company's product lines.

Eventually, this CEO was removed. We were told that the company's 1988 actual losses were $6 million. We would speculate that a variety of other less visible costs were involved, including:

- Opportunity costs caused by the company creating an inherently faulty package instead of the right product
- The long-term reputation of the firm
- The human resources costs in demoralization and turnover

One vice-president we interviewed had witnessed the firing of a bright young woman who criticized the process used to develop the key software package. The CEO stopped the meeting when her concerns were voiced. "She was escorted from the room," the vice-president told us, "and fired within the hour by a VP who was tight with the CEO."

The package the young staff person criticized was released in 1985 and pulled off the market in late 1987 by the new CEO. One vice-president told us, "The program was a disaster. It wouldn't do what we said it would do. There was no ownership, no pride in the product. People were not asked for their input. More energy and time was spent covering your butt than on the quality of the program."

The previous CEO's management style had included such behaviors as:

- Yelling and swearing at people
- Publicly criticizing others
- Not communicating with top staff
- Setting arbitrary deadlines
- Expecting sixty to eighty hours a week from people throughout the organization
- Deliberately pitting vice-presidents against one another

Because of these behaviors, fear was "mirrored all the way down the organization," according to the human resources manager. "It was almost as if the goal was to diminish the individual." The new CEO described the company's employees in the following way:

> 66 *People were scared here. They were like starved children. Their security was threatened. Their self-esteem was damaged. They had lost their belief in themselves and their ability to do quality work. Some people will never really get over that kind of experience, no matter how different I am.* 99

We seldom came across a situation so explicit in its total company impact. Usually it is in smaller, less visible ways that fear's influence accumulates. Declines in morale and dedication and loss of self-esteem usually happen in small increments. In fact, fear is often damaging precisely because of this hidden, incremental quality. It can be taken for granted, like the scrap in a manufacturing process or the inherent waste in many paperwork operations.

Managers often do not see fear's impact dramatically because it is concealed in the process of how the work gets done. As one front-line employee pointed out to us, ours is a result-oriented culture. People do not look at *how;* they only look at *what* and *when* and *how much.* It is a sign of toughness and impatience with bureaucracy and excuses. When one is concentrating on short-term outcomes and the immediate bottom line, it is easy to overlook the long-term loss. For example, when a boss calls employees in to badger them into meeting unrealistic schedules, management often does not see the real problems: how the schedules and project costs were established in the first place, and the real or perceived unwillingness of upper management to hear the true estimates. These issues remain undiscussable and the exhortation to meet the schedule is most likely viewed as a tactic deliberately designed to threaten employees. As such it has the long-term effect of creating greater silence between employees and their bosses.

As fear accumulates in an organization, the *commitment, motivation, confidence,* and *imagination* of individuals are surely diminished. Those are the real costs. It may be argued that such terms are too subjective to measure meaningfully and we would agree. We believe, however, that the reluctance to acknowledge the importance of these intangibles may very well be a sign that the organization has a problem with fear. If organization decision makers look only at the easily determined numbers—whether the engine burns more fuel or less—the environment *for people* may be exactly where the cost efficiencies are lost.

6

BEHAVIORS
THAT
CREATE
FEAR

O ur reality-based field research helped us gain a picture not only of fear's impact, but also of the behaviors that cause fear. After our interviews were completed, we carefully reviewed the situations and experiences for evidence of patterns. This search led us to conclude that there are four major arenas of fear-provoking behaviors. To eliminate fear in an organization ultimately means dealing with each of these arenas. They are:

- Abrasive and abusive conduct by managers and supervisors

- Ambiguous behavior by managers and supervisors

- Poorly managed personnel systems

- The culture of the organization—"how we do things here"—with special emphasis on the performance and conduct of top management

This chapter describes the four categories and how each contributes to a fearful and unproductive work environment. We have organized many of our later remedies to fear according to this framework: Chapter Ten deals extensively with abrasive and abusive conduct; Chapter Twelve addresses ambiguous behavior. However, as we consider abrasive and ambiguous behaviors the more serious and immediate causes of fear, we have concentrated on them in our chapters on strategy.

The four arenas are like concentric circles around a core (see Figure 2). The most frequently cited and visible fear-provoking behaviors are those in the outer rim, abrasive and abusive interpersonal conduct. These create situations in which individuals experience some type of immediate threat. Next is the territory occupied by a manager's ambiguous behavior. Here the threat may not be so obvious. These are more subtle behaviors and potential repercussions which, over time, create a climate conducive to anxiety and fear. Toward the center, experiences with personnel systems stimulate worry about how an individual may be treated in the future. Finally, at the center, the general characteristics of the organization's culture and views of upper management are the least visible. However, they can have a significant influence on the way people react to the three other arenas of fear.

If all of these factors are present on a regular basis, they create a devastating environment. Abrasive and ambiguous conduct from managers, coupled with poorly handled personnel matters and coldness from the top, create a whole world of fear. Our sense is that most of the time only one or two of these pieces are in place, yet the potential is there for all four to be active at once. However, even in more ordinary circumstances, a little bit of fear goes a long way.

By dividing fear-causing behaviors into these four categories, we hope to make them more visible. The arenas we describe often overlap and reinforce one another. An abrasive supervisor who abruptly cuts off a question from an employee about a late performance appraisal

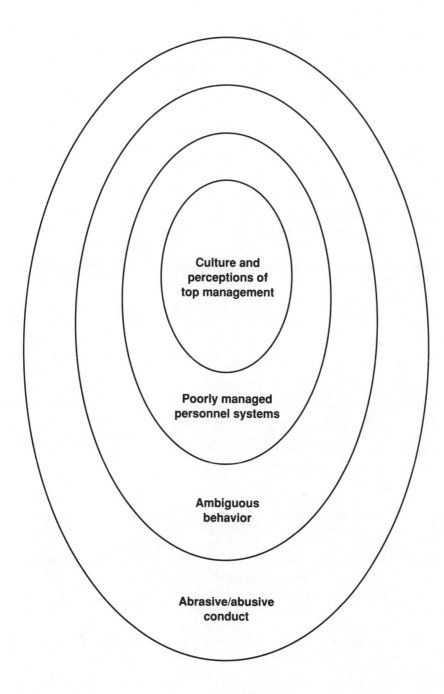

Culture and perceptions of top management

Poorly managed personnel systems

Ambiguous behavior

Abrasive/abusive conduct

Figure 2. Fear Made Visible

is operating in at least three of the four arenas. The distinctions are somewhat artificial, but we think they will help create an understanding of what causes things to go wrong.

ABRASIVE AND ABUSIVE CONDUCT BY MANAGERS AND SUPERVISORS

Perhaps the easiest and most obvious arena to identify is aggressive interpersonal behavior. This consists of obviously intimidating actions. Intentionally or unintentionally, they demean, humiliate, isolate, insult, and threaten people. They range from glaring at someone across a king-sized desk to losing control of one's emotions. More specifically, they include:

- Silence
- Glaring eye contact: "the look"
- Brevity or abruptness
- Snubbing or ignoring people
- Insults and put-downs
- Blaming, discrediting, or discounting
- An aggressive, controlling manner
- Threats about the job
- Yelling and shouting
- Angry outbursts or loss of control
- Physical threats

In addition to the characteristics of the abrasive CEO at the software firm mentioned in Chapter Five, some of the many descriptions of this behavior we heard included:

> 66 [My boss] is someone who leads by intimidation. She yells at staff, talks down to people. She makes blatantly discriminatory comments in front of gay employees. She has no time for people. When you approach her, all you get are short, sharp answers. 99

> —Secretary

66 *Our supervisor crucifies people. She told one employee she was a 'fat slob.' In another situation she screamed at a person whose father had died for not calling in every day. Then when the person came in to pick up her paycheck, she offered the person her performance evaluation. She is formidable, unpredictable, and volatile. She will say things like, 'You'll be in my office at eight o'clock and if you are not here you'll be considered insubordinate.' If you show you are the least bit intimidated, she'll have a field day—crumbling is a sign of weakness.* 99

—Health care professional

66 *Normally, my boss and I would get along well. But if I surprised him with a problem and he had to make a quick decision, he would get red in the face. You could see it creep up his neck. Suddenly, there would be a lot of tension in the air. He'd lose his temper and start shouting.* 99

—Middle manager

Such behaviors immediately destroy trust and end communication. They create a thick wall of antagonism and resentment. No one respects a person who repeatedly puts others down or loses control of his or her temper.

Our sense is that there is a range of these behaviors and that some are more damaging than others. We have created a "gray scale" in Chapter Ten to more fully explore their scope and form a basis for identifying what conduct to avoid. We are convinced that a considerable amount of this behavior is defensive and inadvertent. While a few supervisors certainly *will* use these techniques intentionally, we believe that most bosses do not actually mean to hurt or punish anyone. "I do things I wish I didn't do," one manufacturing boss told us. "Managers are not perfect."

Whether the behaviors are intentional or unintentional, the impact is largely the same: People are very careful around bosses who behave in this way. Their abrasive or abusive patterns create tricky situations for employees. One person told us of his experience with an abrasive boss, "I was advised: 'Look, to handle him, yell back.' But this is not something you experiment with. If you are wrong, you are dead wrong."

These working conditions require an enormous amount of stamina and courage from the employee. Because they are potentially explosive or damaging, it is hard to know what to do to stop the patterns. As a result, the problem frequently goes uncorrected and the boss's style becomes undiscussable. People learn to make do in a fearful environment, never knowing when or where the next abrasive interaction will take place.

AMBIGUOUS BEHAVIOR BY MANAGERS AND SUPERVISORS

Next to abrasive behavior, we believe that ambiguous behaviors cause the most tension for employees. These behaviors are difficult to read. They cause people to wonder what "the rules" are. They leave people confused. Six behaviors surfaced repeatedly in our interviews. The order in which we present them reflects the frequency with which they were mentioned to us. They include ineffective problem solving and decision making; lack of or indirect communication, lack of responsiveness to input or suggestions, inconsistency or mixed messages, uninviting behaviors, and unethical conduct.

Ineffective Problem Solving and Decision Making

This area emerged most often and we consider it particularly important. Individuals in a great many organizations mentioned the impact of ineffective problem-solving or decision-making processes. They frequently singled out *secretive decision making* as provoking fear and mentioned other related problems, such as indecision and failure to explain decisions once they have been made.

Closed-door, behind-the-scenes decision making causes anxiety for several reasons. First, it is regarded as a put-down. Not being included sends the message, "You don't know enough" or "Your judgment isn't valued." Second, not knowing the rationale for decisions makes them especially difficult to implement, thus raising performance fears. Third, if people are not involved in or informed of decisions, their work life becomes unpredictable and open to a range of negative possibilities beyond their influence. They do not know what to expect. These reasons leave people feeling tentative and on edge. This is especially so for those who have a hard time managing ambiguous situations.

In one instance, a human resources staff person described her boss as

> ** very closed door, secretive. She'd close the door with the assistant director. They kept the door closed literally for hours. 'We are in here making plans for the department' was the sense of it. She didn't make decisions. Rather, she seemed to hide behind procedures. She said she was big on teamwork, but it was a joke. There she'd go again into her room with her door closed. **

In another organization, a group of our interviewees talked about "The Unknown," meaning upper management. According to them, "We didn't have a clue where upper management was coming from. We only get the end of it. They are so secretive. Why don't they ask for our advice? Maybe we could *help*."

This is a serious problem area for many organizations because problem solving and decision making are such vital, frequent activities. Chapter Fourteen provides specific advice on how to break down the barriers to effective decision making.

Lack of or Indirect Communication

Indirect or insufficient communication pertains to information that is necessary to do a good job. This includes feedback on performance. Key concerns are

- How much information to share
- Who to share it with
- How to make sure it gets to people in an accurate, timely, and consistent manner

An example of poor information flow comes from one of our consulting experiences. The manager of a branch unit and her chief assistant had developed a serious conflict around who was to have particular information. She felt he did not need certain budget reports and would not pass them along. He failed to give her information about customer complaints. This mutual undermining of the relationship caused anxiety and embarrassment for both sides and exacerbated their long-term conflict. Each had a private interpretation of the other's intent based on this limited flow of information, but neither had expressed these feelings openly. The conflict, while minor, was a symptom of distorted communication that influenced virtually everyone in the organization.

Lack of Responsiveness to Input or Suggestions

When people do not hear back about their suggestions, the door is left open to negative conclusions. They ask themselves questions that reflect confusion and a disquieting combination of mistrust and powerlessness:

66 *Was the idea dismissed?* **99**

❝ *Did upper management find it offensive?* ❞

❝ *Is it worth it to try to improve things around here?* ❞

❝ *Should I ask what happened to my idea?* ❞

❝ *What will they think if I make too big a deal about this?* ❞

These questions lead to doubts and to disappointment that nothing has happened with their ideas. In the absence of other information people often assume the worst. This "worst case" thinking typically promotes both fear and a sense of powerlessness. People worry that because there has been no response to their suggestions, their credibility is being questioned. They hesitate to ask what happened to their ideas for fear of being labeled the "squeaky-wheel troublemaker." They also see the lack of response as more evidence that nothing will change and that there is no use trying to make a difference. We touch on solutions to these problems in two later strategy chapters. In Chapter Eleven, "Value Criticism: Reward the Messenger," we outline actions that encourage people to bring their ideas forward and describe ways to respond appropriately. In Chapter Fifteen, "Challenge Worst-Case Thinking," we explore the phenomenon of worst-case thinking in detail and recommend ways to help overcome this tendency.

Inconsistency or Mixed Messages

When the boss sends a double message or confused signals, people worry. In one case, an administrative support worker discussed how her supervisor gave feedback by talking about the performance or conduct of *other* employees. For example, the supervisor told the worker she would not have to worry that her calls would be monitored to ensure they were all business oriented, "unlike someone else in the office." The employee interpreted this to mean that in fact her calls were being monitored or were in immediate jeopardy of being monitored. Her interpretation was confirmed by a co-worker who had experienced a similar problem with the supervisor. This type of behavior can be extremely intimidating because it leads to a paranoid questioning of all the supervisor's comments—"Is she *really* talking about me?" "What does she *really* mean?"

Many employees also talked to us about "two sets of rules" for managers and employees, as when a decision made by an employee according to policy is overturned at a higher level. These apparent inconsistencies lead people to question their own judgment and feel unclear about how to proceed without losing favor.

Another example is inconsistent reasoning behind decisions. A professional who questioned the hiring decision of a white manager was told that her white appointee had more experience than a competitor from a different racial background. However, in a second selection procedure, the manager argued that another white appointee had been selected because she was not "overqualified," like a second candidate who was a person of color. The two stories increased rather than resolved the employee's concerns about the presence of subtle racism, mixed messages, and double standards.

Uninviting Behaviors

These are behaviors which are not clearly abrasive but are generally cold or aloof. They reflect inattention to the small, but significant and expected, pleasantries and manners associated with human interaction.

- A number of those interviewed commented on the fact that their bosses rarely acknowledged them when they passed in the hall. This lack of common courtesy was taken as the signal of a caste system.

- Even though a manager was highly regarded for his "people" management decisions, his cold "computer-like" intelligence intimidated and confused people. Part of the problem was simply a lack of personal disclosure. Employees did not know "who he was."

- A manager talked and acted fast. Her impatience communicated the message, "How come this isn't done? I told you to do it!" Even though employees recognized that she was simply being impatient and not abrasive or aggressive, the behavior startled and intimidated those who reported to her.

When a manager behaves in a way that can be interpreted as impolite or deliberately distant, the message sets off a line of thinking that goes something like this: "This person does not care about people. Which means that this person probably does not care about me. Which means that I may be in trouble."

Unethical Conduct

This behavior pattern was not frequently mentioned, but people did identify such conduct as outright stealing or embezzling from the company, lying, bragging about drug abuse, and requiring employees to do the boss's personal work on company time. Along with these more extreme examples, we heard about less obvious unethical behavior by managers:

- Claiming an employee's idea as the manager's own
- Playing favorites
- Asking employees not to give complete information to customers

Such behaviors leave employees juggling and sometimes caught between three sets of rules: the company's, their boss's, and their own. The threat of repercussions can hover over their heads from any source—not the least of which is an employee's own personal sense of integrity.

POORLY MANAGED PERSONNEL SYSTEMS

In addition to abrasive and ambiguous behavior, employees worry about how others around them are treated. As one first-line supervisor who had been with her company twenty years put it: "The way another person is treated here equals the way I could be treated. If the company is not loyal to a friend and co-worker, it could happen to me." She expressed this concern because she had watched a top manager who was her friend get "pushed out" of the organization.

Since personnel management systems often control how people are treated, they way these systems operate is of great interest and sometimes great concern to people. A blue-collar worker commented on the hiring process used by a past employer. The company, she said, appeared to be "into an intimidation thing—starting right from the way the initial job interview was set up. It was set up to see how well you could work under pressure."

The signals given off by the way these systems are used tell whether the company supports employees or not. If the affirmative action plan is a "paper document" only, it sends a message. If the compensation program is a "black box" no one can understand and is managed in an apparently inequitable way, it sends a message.

When major personnel management issues surface, such as layoffs, people watch very closely. In a company that was making a shift to a more entrepreneurial business focus, many of the themes centered around how those who had been laid off were treated. This created great anxiety. Survivors of the layoffs commented that their fears were heightened by the following:

- The reasons for the reduction in force (RIF) seemed to relate solely to short-term profits at the expense of the welfare of the organization and its long-term customers.

- There was lack of useful, reassuring follow-up with the survivors.

- The RIF was carried out with an air of secrecy.

- Those who were selected to be laid off were often long-time, well-respected employees.

- The RIF was staggered through departments, so that people were unsure what part of the organization would be hit next and when the RIF would end.

- People were given no warning; they were notified and given almost no time to adjust before being asked to leave.

- There was no obvious effort to place laid-off employees in other positions.

- The names of people to be let go leaked out before they had been officially notified.

How the RIF was carried out became one enormous message about how people were valued by the organization. Given these perceptions, it is no wonder many concluded that management no longer cared about people.

One other aspect of this area is the general reputation of the human resources department. If the department is perceived to be simply an enforcement mechanism or conduit back to line management, employees will worry that seeking advice or counsel will only lead to repercussions. For those with legitimate concerns who need assistance from human resources specialists, this leads to a feeling of being trapped and fearful or alone.

The department's attitude toward people is seen as a symbol of the organization's attitude. For instance, a cold, abrasive human resources director may be seen as a sign that the company does not really care about people. Poor handling of performance, EEO, or career development problems inside the human resources department is a signal to everyone else in the organization that they can expect no help.

Instead employees frequently get the impression that the human resources department—and upper management behind the scenes—is untrustworthy. Human resources can end up being seen as a con by employees. It gives the impression of helping, but in fact it is a trap. As one employee pointed out, "Human resources is a totally Theory X organization. If you went there, the word would get back to your boss before you got back to say you went looking for advice." The burden of human resources, more than any other internal organization, is to live the standard about how people ought to be treated.

THE CULTURE OF THE ORGANIZATION

Many other routine elements of the work environment contribute to fear, particularly those aspects that relate to the conduct and performance of top management. These are often the traditions, habits, and accepted methods of the organization: the "norms" by which it operates. Whether the organizational style is formal or informal, some habits are likely to cause anxiety. Following are examples of tension-creating norms reported by people in our sample:

> " We have an artificial atmosphere that we have to maintain— the dignity of the corporation. We believe our own press clippings. We must always have confidence. "

> " It was the kind of place that supported me-first, aggressive, deceitful behavior. "

> " It was an organization that rewarded put-downs. "

> " People have to prove they can operate in loose structures. People who want a lot of structure become performance problems here. "

> " Around here, if you can't prove it, you don't have the right to say it. "

These patterns create a particular reality for those inside the organization. They are the reference points that teach people how to negotiate the work environment. An organization development manager pointed out to us that with employee orientation, there are always two versions: the official personnel department orientation to the organization and the *real* orientation given by one's peers. The latter is made up of the "Three B's": the benefits of working in the organization, where the bathrooms are, and what to beware of.

An especially important aspect of these norms consist of the stories and perceptions of upper management. We found that even at the entry level, people had a perception of and were concerned about what was happening at the top. In the layoff example used earlier, a significant number of people in the sample commented on the company president's conduct as a fear-provoking element of the RIF. They mentioned the following characteristics:

- He seemed reluctant to answer questions; his responses felt "prompted."

- He did not have the image of a "people person"; he used video-tape and memos to communicate about the RIF, more than actual meetings. He didn't seem as easy to talk to as the previous president, who was someone "you could joke with in the elevator."

- His motives were rumored to be purely ones of financial self-interest; he was attempting to set the company up for a takeover.

These behind-the-scenes beliefs and perceptions reinforced the fears of people throughout the organization. As one survivor put it, "The president is the one person I want to trust, but I don't."

Even without such a dramatic event as layoffs, we often found that people possessed a characterization of upper management. From interview to interview there were consistent themes. In one organization, upper management was considered to be "inconsistent"; in another, "indecisive"; in a third, "arbitrary" or "incompetent." Generally, these opinions were backed up with specific stories that we imagined had traveled freely through the organization's grapevine. Clearly, the words and actions of people at the top set the tone—or undertone—for the way business is done.

In one organization, a first vice-president was reported to have said, "Perception is reality." A lower-level manager assured us that this phrase was a well-known indication of how he expected people to operate. The manager said:

> 66 People lived by that quote. It means, 'If I think it is, it is.' In other words, if something came to his attention, it was true. There would be no investigation. If they hear the bad news at the top, then they will fix blame. 99

In another organization we heard the comment: "It's possible that top managers are competing with one another to build monuments to their areas or to themselves. It's a game of one-upmanship. They are competing for resources."

Needless to say, when top executives have a reputation for being abrasive, this behavior creates a shock wave throughout the organization. People worry about what will happen to them, or to their bosses, if they step out of line. In a few organizations we visited, stories of the angry reactions, put-downs, and threats by the chief executive officer surfaced loudly. Interviewees saw these behaviors as a demonstration of the core values and operating standards of their organization.

Perceptions about top management may have little immediate bearing on day-to-day activities. But like issues with personnel systems, they are a symbol of the way people think they will be treated in the organization. If the perceptions are negative, they create an underlying fear of what the future may hold. If the behaviors employees see from managers are abusive, abrasive, or ambiguous, the patterns of fear become more entrenched. In the next chapter, we offer an explanation of the dynamics that make these behavior patterns so difficult to break.

7

CYCLES OF MISTRUST THAT PERPETUATE FEAR

As we evaluated the data from our interviews, we often asked ourselves about the patterns that keep fear in place. If fear's impact is so important, why have people not naturally discarded the practices that continue its presence? In this chapter we move away from reporting data and theorize how a pattern of entrenched negative assump-

---

tions maintains a *cycle of mistrust*. Understanding why and how supervisors and employees continue to threaten one another lays the foundation for developing a different perspective on work relationships. In Chapter Eight, we will flesh out a positive vision of what relationships can become, in turn creating a platform for the specific strategies used to achieve it.

We believe that it is essential for managers to understand how the cycle of mistrust works. While both bosses and employees share the tremendous responsibility for reversing the pattern of fear, we sense that no progress will be made unless those in leadership positions take the first steps.

SELF-INTEREST, MISTRUST, AND FEAR

The most basic negative assumption which lies at the root of the problems we have described so far is that supervisors and employees do not trust one another. Each side assumes that the other operates from a philosophy of self-interest. Each is expected to try to achieve its self-interest at the expense of the other party. We know that this assumption does not control *all* workplace interactions. In practical terms, supervisors and employees must trust each other to some extent if the work is to get done. But trust is definitely a matter of degree. Even in an otherwise positive relationship, underlying doubts and cautions usually exist which surface easily in times of stress. For example:

> 66 When the conflict occurred, this was the feeling we got from the top: 'Well, we have a problem here between a manager and an employee. Managers are hard to replace—the employee should probably go.' 99
>
> —**Human resources professional**

> 66 They put out messages on the rumor mill that there are going to be layoffs. There probably won't be any layoffs. They just put the rumors out there to get people to work harder. 99
>
> —**Administrative support employee**

> 66 There's a saying around here about retaliation by upper management: 'They may not get back to you right away, but they will get back to you.' 99
>
> —**Financial analyst**

> 66 Our former supervisor—now our manager—doesn't like some-
> one to show him up. He blows up at you; when it's his fault, he
> won't admit it. When he's around me, I'm nervous. I don't know
> what will happen if my current supervisor and I can't figure
> something out and we need to go to him. 99
>
> **—Assembly worker**

Similarly, managers sometimes report manipulation and self-
interest as a theme that ties together their views about employees.

> 66 All this emphasis on feedback for supervisors is just an oppor-
> tunity to 'get your supervisor.' All it does is nurture the bad
> apples who want to get you back. 99
>
> **—Risk manager**

> 66 When people come in the door, it's almost like they lose their
> competence and become people who say 'just tell me what to do. 99
>
> **—Engineering supervisor**

> 66 After a while, I gave up on trying to treat people equally.
> Some people are what I call 'workers.' They are only interested
> in putting in eight hours a day and no more. Why should I treat
> them as though they are special? 99
>
> **—Company owner**

> 66 When are these people going to grow up and stop whining? 99
>
> **—Department director**

At bottom, these comments suggest that when two people have
different levels of organizational power, they cannot fully trust one
another. Employees worry that the boss will ultimately put his or her
own self-interest ahead of the goals of the organization, fair treatment
of customers, and the needs of employees. Supervisors likewise worry
that employees will put their self-interest above the organization, customers, quality, and productivity.

In an environment where comments such as these are heard,
supervisor-employee relationships plateau. The experience is like
having a mild case of the flu. The participants feel mildly sick, yet they
continue with normal routines because they do not feel bad enough
to do what is necessary to get better. In fact, as with coming to work
sick, the illness may gradually worsen. These relationships are suscep-
tible, just waiting for a new policy, organizational change, or other
initiative to create a new outbreak of fear.

THE CYCLE OF MISTRUST

The virus that causes this organizational flu is complex. It combines negative assumptions and self-protective behavior in a self-reinforcing relationship which repeatedly traps both supervisors and employees. The cycle can start anywhere (Figure 3). We have chosen arbitrarily to describe its seven steps beginning with a manager's negative assumptions.

1. *Negative assumptions.*   A manager adopts negative stereotypes based on assumptions about an employee's self-interest and ability to create organizational problems.

2. *Self-protective behavior.*   The manager behaves in ways that are self-protective, acting to defend against the employee's potential to live up to the negative stereotypes.

3. *Observed aggressive behavior.*   The employee sees the manager's self-protective behavior and interprets it to be aggressive and closed.

4. *Reinforced negative assumptions.*   The employee believes that the manager's aggressive behavior is a sign of mistrust and possible manipulation. This reinforces the negative assumptions and stereotypes the employee has about managers.

5. *Self-protective behavior.*   The employee acts in self-protective ways in order to defend against the manager's potential to live up to the negative stereotypes.

6. *Observed aggressive behavior.*   The supervisor sees the employee's self-protective behavior and interprets it to be aggressive and closed.

7. *Reinforced negative assumptions.*   The manager believes that the employee's aggressive behavior is a sign of mistrust and possible manipulation. This reinforces the negative assumptions and stereotypes the supervisor has about employees.

Here is an example of how the cycle might work in a particular situation:

1. *Negative assumptions.*   A new manager has been told by a trusted mentor that employees will "test" decisions and policies

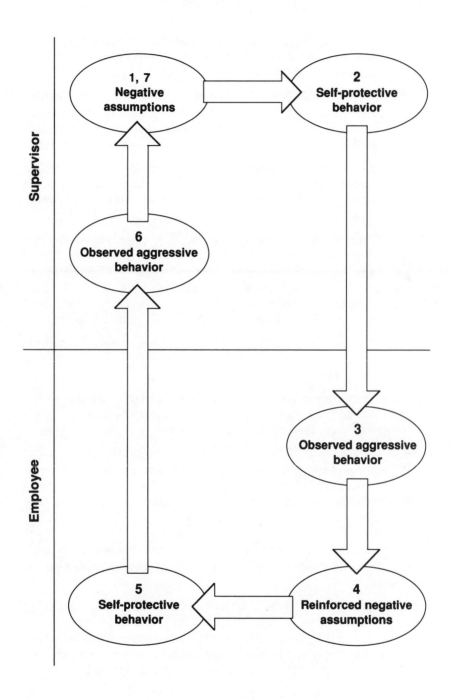

Figure 3. The Cycle of Mistrust

to "see how far they can go." Based upon his own past experience, he believes this can be true. One of his employees is a few minutes late to work twice during the same week.

2. *Self-protective behavior.*   The manager, without investigating, wonders if the employee is testing the policies concerning attendance. He makes a comment at a staff meeting about the importance of attendance and says that he will not tolerate abuse of the rules.

3. *Observed aggressive behavior.*   The employee is surprised by her manager's comments about attendance. She believes that she has been criticized in front of co-workers. She feels embarrassed, angry, and generally insulted.

4. *Reinforced negative assumptions.*   The employee decides that her boss is insecure and is "just power-tripping" on the issue of tardiness. She concludes that her boss is insensitive ("He didn't even ask me why I was late") and has treated her unfairly. She is afraid he will include her tardiness in an upcoming performance appraisal as a way to make her toe the mark.

5. *Self-protective behavior.*   The employee nervously confronts the manager, demanding to know exactly how many minutes late constitute tardiness.

6. *Observed aggressive behavior.*   The manager feels that he has been placed in an uncomfortable position by a defensive and aggressive employee. The employee's question in itself displays a serious lack of accountability.

7. *Reinforced negative assumptions.*   The manager feels reinforced in the belief that employees will test decisions and policies and must be carefully monitored to ensure compliance with the rules.

This cycle happens over and over in many different ways at all levels of organizations characterized by fear. Consider these possible examples:

- Department heads believe that the CEO will operate politically, make decisions behind the scenes, and react defensively to suggestions for change. What self-protective strategies will they adopt in response to these assumptions? How will their behavior look to the CEO, and how will he or she respond?

- A middle manager concludes that first-level supervisors are unwilling to take a big-picture view of their responsibilities.

How will the middle manager act? How will the supervisors see this behavior and how will they act in return?

- Front-line staff and their supervisor are locked into a conflict over deadlines and staffing. The front-line workers believe that quality and safety problems will result from the pressure. The supervisor thinks that the employees are using their concerns as an excuse to make their lives easier. How will each side manage its assumptions and behavior?

NEGATIVE ASSUMPTIONS, SELF-PROTECTIVE STRATEGIES, AND REINFORCING PERCEPTIONS

In order to make this cycle of mistrust more vivid, we have catalogued for both managers and employees lists of negative assumptions, self-protective strategies, and reinforcing perceptions. We know that such lists can easily be glossed over rather than read slowly and carefully. We encourage careful consideration of each of the items presented here, which relate to the points on the cycle. As you read them, think about your experiences as a boss and as an employee. Which items have been part of your behavior or beliefs? To what degree have you contributed to or been trapped by the cycle of mistrust?

Negative Assumptions Managers Make About Employees (Point 1)

Employees

- Do not take accountability
- Do not really care about their work beyond getting their paycheck
- Are unwilling to look at a big-picture view
- Look for excuses
- Test policies and rules
- Need structure, control, and limits in order to stay focused

- Will not contribute unless they are forced to do so
- Do not understand political realities and budgetary pressures, and are unwilling to do so
- Focus on rights, benefits, money, and other "entitlements"
- Are capable of dishonesty and sabotage

Self-Protective Strategies Adopted by Managers (Point 2)

Managers will therefore

- Micro-manage employees' work
- Restrict participation in policy or other important workplace decisions
- Institute new performance standards that focus on commitment, attitude, and loyalty
- Emphasize a formal chain of command for handling employees' complaints or suggestions
- Develop tighter personnel rules
- Limit the information communicated to employees
- Transfer or reassign people
- Take, or attempt to take, disciplinary action with employees who appear to be causing trouble for management
- Restrict meetings to upper-management groups
- Nip dissent in the bud
- Come down hard on people who are screwing up as an example to others
- Criticize employees; hold them up to ridicule
- Focus on their "rights" as supervisors

How These Self-Protective Strategies Look to Employees (Point 3)

Employees see

- Two sets of rules—one for managers, one for employees

- Employees transferred, reassigned, or terminated without explanation or apparent rationale
- Rumors about possible changes in the work, layoffs, or reorganization without confirmation or denial by management
- Announcements of new rules that restrict behavior without input or explanation
- Closed-door meetings by managers
- Managers' actions not corresponding with stated fair treatment policies on promotions, training, appraisals, EEO matters, or other human resources issues
- Warnings by managers to employees not to take their complaints or suggestions higher in the organization
- The immediate supervisor being the only person allowed to take good ideas to higher levels of management
- Managers who think that ridiculing, harassing, or punishing employees is acceptable

Negative Assumptions Employees Make About Managers as a Result (Point 4)

Managers

- Are insensitive to the personal life and legitimate needs, rights, and interests of employees
- Are secretive about motives and decisions; operate behind the scenes
- Have as their biggest interest personal control and power; use organizational power to achieve private ends
- Operate as a privileged elite, a closed club that creates a "caste system" in the organization
- Continuously try to get more work out of employees with no additional rewards
- Play politics; are more interested in politically correct solutions than technically correct ones
- Show favoritism and bias
- Are defensive about ideas they did not generate themselves

- Ask for input as a sop to employees' emotions, but are never really influenced by employees' ideas or interests
- Are insecure and threatened by competent employees
- Will do whatever they need to do to promote their own careers
- Think that they are better than employees with less power
- Are dishonest and capable of hidden retaliation

Self-Protective Strategies Adopted by Employees (Point 5)

Employees will therefore

- Openly suggest that management or particular managers are incompetent
- Prevent information and data from flowing up the system
- Allow a manager to make mistakes in front of the manager's supervisors or peers
- Blame others or circumstances for performance problems
- Ask for more money or better working conditions
- Joke about or make fun of the manager with co-workers
- Challenge all management decisions
- Complain to vendors or competitors about the organization's problems
- Not contribute at meetings, but complain about them afterward
- Refuse to do overtime work required by an urgent issue or problem
- Seldom acknowledge their own contribution to a problem situation
- Fail to inform managers of pertinent stories on the rumor mill
- Send grievance petitions to high-ranking or influential people
- Form a union; focus on their "rights" as employees
- File a legal complaint or lawsuit

How These Self-Protective Strategies Look to Managers (Point 6)

Managers see

- Excessive time spent resisting reasonable requests; a general lack of cooperation
- Excuses; people not taking responsibility for problems they have caused or could correct
- Employees not giving the organization a reasonable chance to correct problems
- Requests for personal leaves or other benefits that will slow down the work
- Considerable time spent with co-workers complaining and "whining"
- A lack of new ideas to improve the product or service
- Frequent requests for new benefits
- Petty complaints represented as serious organizational problems
- Statements which do not support the organization and its customers
- People not working up to their potential
- Aggressiveness
- People working the system for personal gain

RECIPROCAL SELF-PROTECTIVE STRATEGIES

The negative images managers and employees have of one another frequently are of a reciprocal nature. These mirror images often result in self-protective strategies which follow the same general trends. Both sides engage in such activities as

- Blaming
- Making excuses
- Restricting the flow of information
- Restricting participation in important decisions

- Creating us/them distinctions
- Reinforcing mandated structures, authority, and rights
- Discrediting others' competence and willingness to take responsibility
- Undermining or sabotaging others' efforts
- Expressing cynicism

The last strategy employed by managers and employees deserves special comment. Cynicism, in blanket form, communicates that self-interest is behind all important decisions and actions. It is a most powerful lock that helps keep the cycle of mistrust in operation. Cynicism makes fear and a sense of powerlessness total certainties. It drives individuals to become negative "realists" about human nature and about work. Not being cynical is held to be naive. Not speaking up becomes the "smart" way to operate. Trusting that a boss or a subordinate might actually have your best interest in mind is considered stupid.

As with undiscussables, these and other similar behaviors are both the cause and result of fear. They are typically read by the other side as offensive rather than defensive. The reciprocal quality of the conduct means that managers and employees are engaged in a continuous, usually low-key, conflict. Sometimes, as in adversarial labor-management situations, the conflict is played out dramatically. More often it hides beneath the surface of events, subtly influencing emotions and behavior.

It is clear that some people feel the cycle of mistrust more strongly and deeply than others. Their actions implicitly express its assumptions and self-protective strategies. Once, for example, when we were presenting the cycle as part of a management training class, one of the participants commented that he thought the term "assumptions" was inaccurate. He told us that "facts" was the better word. His response exactly highlights the problem with the cycle of mistrust. When people believe in the stereotypical view of bosses and employees upon which the cycle is based, the conflict is certain to continue.

TRIGGERING THE CYCLE WITH UNRELATED BEHAVIORS AND EVENTS

It should be noted that the examples of self-protective behaviors and reciprocal strategies presented in this chapter are similar to, but not quite the same as, the behaviors that cause fear which were listed in the previous chapter. This is an important point. We believe that the behaviors described for each of the four arenas in Chapter Six *trigger* the cycle. But the behaviors themselves may not necessarily be based on the cycle. Ambiguous behavior, such as lack of follow-up to a subordinate's work suggestion, may not be grounded in negative beliefs about employees at all. But for the employee, it confirms a negative assumption about the insensitivity of supervisors. An employee's termination may be a totally justified and appropriate action based on placement and skills, but others are likely to become fearful. In other words, actions by management or employees that look like they might be part of a cycle of mistrust, or that leave room for interpretation, are often concluded to be so.

This hit home for us while interviewing a supervisor who terminated one of his employees. He explained,

> 66 When I took over as boss there was an older woman in my group who was not performing. I set forth expectations for her performance with clear statements of rewards and punishments. I was, however, never able to help her. She was afraid and became fatalistic. I worried that her two co-workers would be scared, and in fact one of the two was very worried. She and I talked for three hours one night. She wanted to know whether I was there to fix the problem or just set unrealistic goals. 99

We also had an opportunity to interview the co-worker:

> 66 I sympathized [with the woman who would later be terminated], but I also realized that improvements were necessary. I tried to be positive about her and help her implement the needed changes in her performance. There was a lot of stress and tension in our group. It made it hard to concentrate on my job. The quality of my work probably was reduced.
>
> 66 While I felt the supervisor was correct in handling the situation, it was hard not to side with my co-worker. The situation made me suspicious of my supervisor. He was new to our area and within nine months he had terminated my co-worker. There was a question of whether the supervisor had come into our area with his mind made up to get rid of her or to work with her performance. 99

These two versions of the same event show how people's fears can intrude, even when the supervisory action is understood to be appropriate. The cycle of mistrust can be heard in the employee's question: Did he have his mind made up to get rid of her? It was significant to us that both people identified this situation as currently undiscussable. Neither was inclined to reopen the conversation and talk about their experiences and emotions. This means that there is little chance to resolve these leftover frustrations and fears. It was clear to us that the supervisor felt ineffective with his employee. Conversely, the employee continued to worry about what her co-worker's termination meant regarding her boss's methods.

We believe that in this situation the supervisor needs to find a way to gently reopen the issue. He should demonstrate his willingness to hear his employee's fears about his motivation and respond nondefensively. The employee needs to know that the termination was not just an outcome of the assumptions that underlie the cycle of mistrust. In this way, the incident actually becomes an opportunity for building honesty and trust. Left undiscussed, the matter could easily feed a belief that managers are secretive about their motives and employees are unable to see the big picture or let go of their fears. The lesson is that managers

- Need to do their best to avoid the fear-provoking behaviors described in the previous chapter
- Should stay away from making negative assumptions about their employees
- Should realize that workplace changes, no matter how justified, may cause the cycle to surface

WHAT KIND OF A WORKPLACE IS THIS?

The picture we have drawn in this and preceding chapters is not a pretty one. The cycle of mistrust is self-perpetuating. The framework of threatening behaviors and practices suggests that almost every aspect of the organization can be touched by fear. The lists of negative assumptions, self-protective behaviors, and possible negative interpretations of those behaviors seem endless. Words like *retaliation, sabotage,* and *dishonesty* are not pleasant to consider.

For those who think we paint too bleak a picture, we can only say that the cycle of mistrust has been present at some level in all the organizations in our experience. Often it has been like background noise, going unnoticed until it significantly interferes with people's ability to communicate. We believe that organizations are filled with managers and employees who have grown accustomed to living with a certain level of mistrust, cynicism, and fear. They are habituated to unsatisfying relationships that manage to crank out the work and maintain the status quo. They are ready to have their worst assumptions proven true. Even when opportunities for positive change present themselves, people believe that things cannot be improved. Their negative assumptions too easily become their reality.

The cycle of mistrust, of course, is not the whole picture. The fear that inhabits the background of organizational life is counterbalanced by the talents, positive experiences, and hopeful ideals of people. We now shift to an optimistic view of the possibilities in Part III, describing in detail the strategies to reduce fear. The disquieting journey of past chapters—from undiscussables and repercussions to the cycle of mistrust—becomes the impetus behind a powerful and exciting vision for working relationships.

PART THREE

■

STRATEGIES FOR A HIGH-TRUST WORK ENVIRONMENT

8

BUILD RELATIONSHIPS WITHOUT FEAR

At the same time that people perpetuate a degree of mistrust, they maintain hopes for a brighter reality. Throughout our research, we did not meet a single person who did not want his or her organization to be successful. People want to do a good job and be proud of their work. They want to contribute to a success that is greater than their own. They want to have good working relationships and feel respected as competent employees and valuable individuals. They do not wake up in the morning planning ways to make someone else's life miserable. Even those who are known for their cynical view of life will acknowledge that while they think it may be highly unlikely, they would like to see things improve.

Just as managers and employees have the capacity to negatively affect each other's lives, they possess a similar potential to positively contribute to one another's success. In order for this positive potential to work, people must examine and discard the old patterns of mistrust and cynicism. Their instinctive habits of making negative assumptions about each other must be broken.

While changing habits is never easy, there is an enormous payoff. People begin to feel great about their work. Energy, creativity, and quality improve. As fear diminishes, trust and confidence find room to grow. Time spent complaining, worrying, rehearsing, and dealing with emotional stress can be redirected toward accomplishing goals.

THE NEW VISION

The first step in moving away from the fears described in the last seven chapters is to understand a new vision of workplace relationships. To do so, we have involved over 300 people during the last three years. In a variety of small groups, we have asked them to define their idea of a great working relationship. Since, for many, differences in organizational power complicate this vision, we have focused the discussion on outstanding *co-worker* relationships. This approach helps people concentrate on the characteristics of the relationship rather than on differences in authority.

People spontaneously generate long lists of qualities they personally have experienced in satisfying co-worker relationships. Within ten minutes, groups can list twenty or thirty characteristics. Commonly cited qualities are

- Mutual helpfulness, understanding, and trust
- Serving as a reality check for one another
- Providing feedback for one another—on strengths as well as areas that need improvement
- Influencing each other's ideas and decisions; willingness to be influenced
- Humor; enjoyment of each other's company

- Creative, synergistic problem solving where the results are greater than the sum of the parts

- Respect for different backgrounds and talents; reliance on each other's expertise

- Willingness and ability to work through conflicts and disagreements

- Common commitment to the same goal; commitment to each other's success

- A high level of rapport and honesty with one another

- Straightforward communication

These qualities suggest an interpersonal relationship which genuinely supports the performance and success of both people. We call these qualities *core behaviors* because they form the basis for excellent work relationships, regardless of hierarchical levels. They describe partnership and teamwork at their best: individuals doing high-quality work directed toward common goals and achieving personal satisfaction at the same time.

In such relationships, there are strong feelings of trust. Collaboration is seen as a joyful, positive thing, even when it includes or has been generated by disagreement. When undiscussable issues are discovered, they are quickly brought to the surface. Conflicts and negative feedback, while still painful, are recognized as a powerful source of mutual learning and growth. People can be vulnerable with one another and confident that their interpersonal risks will pay off.

Such relationships clearly contribute to the development of each person's competence and sense of personal well-being. At their best, they include a high level of rapport and mutual understanding which gives work a special sense of purpose and value. The high quality of this partnership and the high quality of the work produced are inseparable.

When a manager-employee hierarchy is introduced, these core behaviors can and should remain the same. Instead of drifting off toward defensive behavior or avoidance, each person communicates in a straightforward manner and is equally committed to the task and to each other's success. The manager and employee behave as co-workers with different areas of expertise and accountability. For example, the manager's responsibility usually includes having the final say on key decisions and making sure that each employee has the necessary resources and training to successfully complete assigned tasks. The employee typically attends to a more detailed level of operations and keeps the manager informed about both problems and successes. Each knows that mutual success depends on his or her ability to perform tasks, make decisions, solve problems, and keep the other person informed.

The point is that differences in formal hierarchical power do not need to alter negatively the quality of the relationship between people—one of whom happens to work for the other. Each has a specific area of expertise, role, and area of accountability. Each is dependent on the other to be successful in the organization. This does not mean that everything moves along in a perfectly smooth manner. When hard times hit and conflict emerges, people work together to deal with the issues. In a hierarchy they do this across the boundaries of formal power, just as co-workers cross boundaries of different backgrounds, perspectives, and technical skills.

This vision of workplace relationships represents a significant shift from models that emphasize control, separation of functions, and authority differences. Interdependence and cooperation between individuals—be they boss, employee, or peers—are essential to success. For the manager and the employee, this vision defines a level of equality in which both flourish. When people know that they are fully and equally committed to one another's success, there is no room for fear to exist.

RELATIONSHIPS BETWEEN A BOSS AND A SUBORDINATE

Some people tell us that this vision may be fine for co-workers, but that it will have a tough time being accepted by managers and employees in "the real world." They typically say something like, "This is a great idea, but . . . " In their "buts," they bring up an important question: How can a boss and subordinate have the type of relationship described in the vision when it is obvious that the boss has a lot more power?

Managers' organizational power is based upon their greater level of decision-making accountability. Within their areas of responsibility are, of course, the ability to evaluate performance, hire, fire, promote, demote, and change employee assignments and roles. Managers at all levels have a larger scope than their subordinates. They typically have more responsibility for larger numbers of resources. They oversee a greater number of functions. With closer access to the top of the organization, they usually get information from higher levels before their employees and have greater personal influence on the direction of the organization. Employees have a smaller and more focused area of decision making. Whether they are workers on the shop floor or vice-presidents in executive suites, they still have a smaller scope of decision-making authority than do their bosses. And, obviously, they do not personally have the formal authority to hire, fire, promote, or demote their bosses.

The slippery point here is that differences in decision-making authority do not mean that supervisors and employees must inevitably give up on the vision we have described. The cycle of mistrust emerges when supervisors and employees connect their differences in organizational authority with their potential to negatively affect one another's lives. This negative, power-oriented focus often causes people—both managers and employees—to feel threatened. Fernando Bartolomé and André Laurent (1986) documented this dynamic with a study of over 100 executives. While their work concentrated on people in mid-level and senior management positions, we believe the pattern holds true throughout an organizational hierarchy. They observe that

> managers as superiors know how much they depend on their subordinates' performance and, therefore, how much real power, as opposed to formal power, their subordinates have over them. But when bosses are subordinates, they often forget this reality of organizational life. They forget that their boss's performance depends heavily on how committed the subordinates are to their jobs and on the quality of their work. . . . They don't always recognize that they possess real power that they can use with their bosses to negotiate and obtain satisfaction for their legitimate needs and demands [p. 80].

When managers and employees talk about this relative balance of power, they will most often cite negative examples to prove their points. Employees will talk about how a boss can disrupt their lives by a sarcastic comment, an unwanted assignment, a critical comment, or a poor performance appraisal. Managers will tell stories about uncaring staff, operational information that was negligently delayed, and the unwillingness of employees to take the initiative to solve problems on the spot. It is clear that if the goal is to make another person's life miserable, each has the ability to be quite successful. It is like two boxers in a ring. One may weigh twenty pounds more than the other, but that is no guarantee that both will not be bloodied by the time the match is over.

Instead, when people—whether they are co-workers or managers and employees—adhere to the core behaviors, their concerns about these power differences disappear. Employees in such relationships will say things like "Of course my boss has greater decision-making authority than I do—and that's fine." Because people are tuned into their common goals and their commitment to each other's success, power becomes a non-issue, except when it can be used to help others be more successful. When people start worrying about their different levels of power, control, or decision-making authority, it is a sure sign that the negative assumptions have crept into their thinking.

PUTTING THE CORE BEHAVIORS TO WORK

When peers or managers and employees function according to the core behaviors, they completely reverse the reciprocal self-protective strategies that are a part of the cycle of mistrust. Their undiscussables disappear, and new opportunities for business success and professional development emerge. When this happens within the context of a manager-employee relationship, it is especially heartening—given the cynicism and mistrust that typifies so many of those relationships. People of different authority levels can, and do, behave in the following ways:

1. Instead of blaming each other, they give credit for good work that is being done. Bosses and subordinates publicly acknowledge each other's hard work, strengths, and original ideas. Employees are encouraged to express their ideas and be visible to top leadership. On the other hand, employees talk about how the boss's insight or technical skill helps them be successful. Both talk about how much they learn from working together and let each other know how much they—and their work—are appreciated.

2. People take responsibility rather than making excuses. Supervisors and employees alike admit when they make mistakes. They identify problems early so that others are warned of potential difficulties. They take initiative in offering solutions, pulling people and other resources together to correct difficult situations. They believe that if people do not make mistakes, they never will improve. They support each other when mistakes are made and help each other figure out how to do things differently in the future.

3. Information is shared rather than restricted. Information related to decisions, rumors, events, and technical developments is passed easily between employees and managers and back again. They both believe that accurate and timely information is essential to anyone doing quality work. They are committed to keeping each other informed. They know that not all information can or should be exchanged. Both employees and managers trust each other to pass along information appropriately. If they do not get the information they need, they talk to each other and set plans in motion that will prevent problems in the future.

4. People collaborate on important issues. Managers and employees are sensitive to the way their decisions influence one another. They seek each other's opinions and expertise. When it is practical, decisions are made by consensus. People speak up and fully participate in offering their views. If decision making must be top-down, managers explain why this is so, share the reasoning behind the decision, and explain how employee input was used. By the same token, employees seek their managers' views and support on sensitive decisions that fall within their areas of accountability.

5. Instead of creating "us and them" distinctions, people talk in terms of "we." In spirit, people assume that "we're all in this together." They see success, failure, learning, and problem solving as issues of mutual concern. They think about how their own roles and behaviors affect others and the organization at large. Without regard for the power differences between them, bosses and subordinates believe that their job is to make sure the other is successful.

6. People focus on the big-picture issues and do not get sidetracked by differences in the details. Employees and managers keep their collective mission in mind. They acknowledge their differences regarding details and figure out how to work with them. They recognize the real issue: "How do we move forward together to accomplish what we both believe is important?"

7. People respect organizational structures and roles and do not use them as weapons. Instead, whatever the role, they mutually try to make sure that decisions are correct, information is exchanged, and conflicts are attended to constructively. People do not talk about their "rights" or their turf. They decide together what is right in a particular situation.

8. Rather than discrediting each other's competence, employees and managers value each other's background and experience. People

seek each other's opinions because they have learned that "one plus one equals more than two." The synergistic effects of combining viewpoints and expertise lead to better-quality work. They ask each other questions like "What have I forgotten here?" or "How would you approach this problem?" Because people think and talk in terms of "we," they do not say or do things that would deliberately discredit anyone. They value diversity and speak positively of one another's contributions to others in the organization.

9. Concerns, criticisms, and conflicts are openly voiced. Neither employees nor managers act in ways that would undermine, manipulate, or sabotage each other's efforts. Because of commitments to common goals, most disagreements and conflicts relate to methods of accomplishing work. When these arise, they are discussed openly. People say what they think and trust that the other person will not take criticisms personally. They give each other critical feedback that will help improve individual and collective performance. They do not worry about "getting paid back" for suggesting different approaches or a different line of reasoning. If that concern should ever come up, it would be discussed directly. In response to the feedback, people listen carefully and do their best to respond to each other's concerns. They see their ability to disagree and manage their conflicts as a strength of their relationship.

10. Rather than expressing cynicism, employees and managers speak positively about their work, the organization, and the future. This does not mean that they avoid problems. Dilemmas are identified and talked about in realistic ways that help people move forward. Uncertainties and the impact of changes in industry, technology, and the environment are discussed openly and positively. People are encouraged to express their concerns, frustrations, discouragement, confusion, and anger. Acknowledgment of these feelings is considered an important step toward managing change. "Can-do" attitudes prevail because people target their actions in arenas that they can actually influence.

The core behaviors represent a shared interpersonal goal. When people operate with this goal, while fully acknowledging the differences in their organizational roles and decision-making authority, they search for ways to make these differences complementary rather than adversarial. That is, they search for ways to build on each other's professional and operational strengths, rather than competing with one another or playing on each other's weaknesses. When a boss and subordinate are able to relate to one another in this way, they make it easier for co-workers to experience this same high-quality, high-performance relationship.

While it may be difficult to achieve this goal, sharing it creates a kind of interpersonal and professional glue. Once that glue is in place, there are few barriers to solving problems. The curtain of mistrust that separates managers and employees comes down. People become proud of their ability to give feedback openly and to accept it from others. They become excited about their ability to learn from one another and work together to accomplish a greater purpose.

If they are allowed to grow, the core behaviors create a direction for high-performance relationships. In such cases, high performance becomes both a means and an end. It defines the quality of the inter-action between a manager and an employee as well as the quality of the work they produce together. Once they have been established, these relationships both require and reinforce trust, creativity, risk taking, and commitment. They become their own positive self-perpetuating cycle—a cycle that has no room for fear or time for mistrust.

Does this vision of the supervisor-employee relationship create too high a standard? We think not. Can such relationships ever be achieved? Our research and experience tell us that they already exist. While they are currently in the minority, such relationships are essential if organizations are ever going to move beyond current patterns of mistrust and fear.

THE KEY IS CHANGING ASSUMPTIONS

Just as the cycle of mistrust is based on negative assumptions, the vision we have described is based on positive ones. If people begin with the premise that they can trust one another, their work relationships take on a new dimension. We sense that high-trust relationships are where virtually everyone wants to be. But the world is full of systems, manage-ment philosophies, assumptions, and a horde of interpersonal barriers that keep us from achieving this goal. We do not accept that the nega-tive assumptions of the cycle of mistrust are an essential part of human nature. On the contrary, we believe that the mistrust we have described is basically unnatural. While conflicts and disagreements are inevitable, the underlying tone of organizations does not have to be one of fear. People want, need, and can obtain supportive relationships at work.

As a first step, individuals can challenge the negative assumptions about employees and managers that are reinforced by the cycle of mistrust. Suppose, for example, managers assumed that employees

- Want to take responsibility for their work and want to do a good job
- Care about their work above and beyond the money they get paid to perform it
- Consider a big-picture view essential to performing their work
- Are willing to take responsibility for their mistakes
- Are capable of establishing their own structures in order to maintain focus
- Want to contribute freely
- Are fully capable of understanding budgetary and political realities
- Do not just focus on their entitlements and rights
- Are intrinsically honest and trustworthy

Next, consider what might happen if employees believed that managers

- Are sensitive to the personal issues and interests of employees
- Enjoy open, participative problem solving
- Want to use the power of their station to serve the organization well, and consider it unethical to use power to achieve private ends
- Want the workload to be fair and reasonable
- Work to find solutions that are both technically and politically sound
- Pride themselves on operating fairly and objectively
- Want their input on decisions
- Are willing to put the success of the organization, welfare of the employees, and service to customers before private interests
- Do not think they are better than their employees
- Are honest and would consider retaliation a sign of serious weakness

We sense that these sets of assumptions are much closer to reality than many managers and employees believe. The problem is that people do not think that the other side is trying to behave this way, too. All too often individuals make positive assumptions about themselves but negative ones about the others, whoever they are. This "good guys and bad guys" perspective is read by the other side as an unspoken but real set of negative assumptions that must be defended against. Each group believes that the other wants radically different things. Yet time after time in conflict management and team-building work, the answer comes back that everybody wants the same things: respect, participation, a voice, clarity, fairness, understanding, common goals, a meaningful job, and opportunities to achieve something worthwhile. Jerry Harvey makes this point in memorable fashion in *The Abilene Paradox*. He asserts that it is the inability to manage our agreements— not our disagreements—that gets us into trouble (1988, p. 15).

Although the cycle of mistrust would have people think differently, we basically believe that people all want very much the same things. We want to underscore our belief that human connections are much more powerful than organizational ones. Things get done because of relationships between people, not because job descriptions are well thought out and explicit. It is not that organizational roles and structures are unimportant. In some form they are essential. It is just that they can never be a substitute for the core behaviors. As we have learned, organizations may be able to get someone to do a job, but that person will not, and cannot, do more than the basics without an environment of trust, credibility, and opportunity.

EASY TO SAY, HARDER TO DO

Taking a positive view of the "other side" can be tough to carry out because of people's self-focused belief that they know reality and understand others' motives. To build a relationship based upon the vision we have presented here takes time and hard work. Such relationships grow piece by piece, building from small interactions between people. In order for people to realize their hopes for these relationships, they need to set aside years of conditioning about what it is like to work for a boss, supervise an employee, or compete with a co-worker. They need to discard, override, and reject the cycle of mistrust. None of this is easy.

The remaining chapters in this section present seven major strategies that leaders can use to replace fear and mistrust with energy and innovation. They are intended to answer the questions, "As manager, how do I get started achieving this vision?'' and ''How do I go about overcoming patterns of fear?'' Each of the strategies contributes to the type of relationships described in this chapter. And, predictably, each reflects many of the actions bosses can take to encourage people to speak up about their concerns.

The strategies reflect a range from highly structured and concrete steps, where the manager may play a role typical of traditional hierarchies, to somewhat more abstract group-oriented approaches, where the leader serves as a facilitator and agent of change. This variety offers a choice of starting points and comfort zones.

Our approach is an eclectic one. All the strategies aim to reduce fear as a barrier between people who need to work together. They come at fear from many different angles. Some of them are new. Most are based on familiar principles of sound personnel management or organization development efforts. A number represent a straightforward, commonsense approach to human relations problems.

Some of the strategies require considerable effort and personal or interpersonal risk taking. The work of reducing fear calls for courage. We suggest that you think carefully about the levels of risk and tension you are ready to take on. Select strategies which will cause you to stretch, but do not push yourself into an arena you are not prepared to handle.

We frequently suggest basic approaches because they are often the ones most neglected. As people search for powerful tools to help them facilitate organizational change, manage conflicts, and empower others, practical first steps are often overlooked. Major changes and broad programs are sometimes appropriate, but often working on the details of interactions and relationships is the most powerful work a manager can do.

In our experience, the broad, flashier approach tends to be found alongside a general philosophy of impatience and short-term thinking. This tendency reflects a misunderstanding of how people-management initiatives work best. Too often such initiatives are approached like engineering projects—as a planned, logical sequence of steps with a designated budget and time frame and quantifiable outcomes.

Our view is that the culture and relationship changes suggested in this book are not amenable to being implemented in this way. Rather, they are likely to occur as an exhilarating but messy, often excruciatingly slow learning process in which mistakes and dilemmas are frequent. These unexpected, sometimes disappointing outcomes are not signals that the method is a failure or the intention is wrong. Rather they should be taken as catalysts to new understandings and additional steps. Reducing fear is a long and winding road.

As a consequence, we have tried to break the strategies into bite-sized pieces and often include action steps that may seem to some superficial or overly simple. We hope that, whatever your level of managerial sophistication, you will take the time to read through and carefully consider your performance on these basic steps. We believe that slowing down to consider these actions will help you to refocus your attention on what you already know is right in working with others.

SKILLS REQUIRED OF MANAGERS

To carry out any of these strategies a manager must behave in certain ways:

1. Demonstrate that you are listening. Listen accurately to what others are saying. This means that you need to be able to paraphrase, respond to people's emotions, and pay attention to nonverbal body language and tone of voice.

2. Serve as a role model. Be willing to do what you ask others to do. For example, you should work at eliminating abrasive behavior personally if you are asking others to abide by a similar standard. If you want others to discuss sensitive issues, show a willingness to discuss such topics yourself.

3. Be an initiator. Take the lead in turning fear into trust. It is clear that in order for any relationship to improve, both or all parties need to be actively involved. However, your formal or informal leadership position—not to mention your interest in the subject of this book—enables you to more effectively take the first step. Act on some of what we suggest in the following chapters.

4. Be open to feedback. You will need to be able to accept sensitive feedback about your own communication and leadership style. In fact, you should be on a continuous hunt to track down feedback about how you come across. Willingness to accept personal feedback is a critical element of being able to reward—rather than shoot—the messengers.

5. Be willing to make personal changes. Be open to adjusting personal behavior as a result of feedback or other learning. The strategies, particularly the later ones, require energy, commitment, and

follow-through in order to achieve results. They may well push you to change ingrained habits. You will be ineffective as a role model for others unless you demonstrate your willingness to do things differently.

6. Be vigilant. Be alert to the real-world opportunities that emerge as part of the organization's work. Stay in touch with the work environment and observe the behaviors of others. You should always be prepared to use what is happening day to day as a chance to apply the ideas and work through the problems related to fear.

7. Deal with your own fear of speaking up. If you seldom hesitate, think about times in your life when you did. Use your own experience to learn about and appreciate the vulnerabilities of others.

8. Facilitate, rather than direct, discussions and meetings. Be a catalyst for others' discussion and reflection. Communicate in ways that encourage others to offer their views. Pay attention to *how* things get done, making sure that information flow, decision making, and follow-up actions are understood by all participants and are open to influence.

9. Take a developmental, learning-oriented approach. See the experience of reducing fear as a way to create new insights for yourself and others. Do not be afraid to make some mistakes as you proceed, and accept the inevitable adjustments and changes to the process as part of a natural learning curve.

10. Bring in an outside consultant. When you feel that you are in over your head with interpersonal or group dynamics, seek the services of an outside consultant. Outside facilitation will enable you to be a full participant in the problem-solving process rather than trying to play the roles of leader, participant, and facilitator at the same time.

In themselves, these skills represent a high standard for managerial conduct. We believe that the pursuit of these behaviors through thought and practice can move manager-employee relations a long way toward the core behaviors. When put to use through the strategies described in the next seven chapters, the result can be a whole new kind of relationship between bosses and their employees.

9

ACKNOWLEDGE

THE

PRESENCE

OF FEAR

As with any process of change, people are likely to go through a series of stages in their understanding of fear and their commitment to reversing its negative patterns. These can be diagramed as shown in Figure 4. This chapter is specifically focused around the first three steps of the scale. It highlights the importance of early work that builds

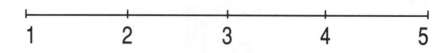

1   Lacking awareness or denial
2   Seeking information and listening
3   Recognizing the problem in one's own environment
4   Developing a plan of action
5   Carrying out that plan

Figure 4.   Points of Awareness and Action

awareness and overcomes denial. Like other workplace changes, making a course correction around fear requires that people understand the problem and see it happening around them. Once fear's presence has been acknowledged, planning for and implementing a new course of action can begin.

START SMALL AND GO SLOWLY

Getting everybody into the pool usually requires someone to test the water first. The manager's role is to tell others, "Hey, the water's fine, let's get in." This does not mean that you must be a technical expert on either water quality or swimming. With fear, the first goal is usually to get others talking about it. To do so, you can begin by voicing your own concerns about fear and its effects. Model the level of openness about this topic that you would like to achieve with others. Do not feel you need to have all the answers. You may wish to include the following techniques:

1. Focus initially on the fear of speaking up. Pick simple ways to do this. A newspaper article about employee involvement or other workplace innovations can be a catalyst to discussion. Generate conversation around barriers companies face in getting people to identify needed improvements. If it does not automatically surface, add the fear of repercussions to the list of barriers and ask people to describe their related experiences.

2. Show them this book. Share the definitions and some conclusions you find interesting.

3. Tell stories from your own experience, preferably ones from other organizations. You might say, "I once worked for somebody who had the habit of talking down to employees. It sure was annoying, and it scared the heck out of people who didn't know him well." Ask if anybody else has had a similar experience. Set a personal direction and ask for their help. "I want to avoid making the same mistake. I hope you will tell me if I ever come across that way."

This process of planting seeds is an informal one, woven into day-to-day interactions. It gets people thinking and lets them know where *you* are coming from. Along the way you get a chance to practice the vocabulary of fear—words such as *scared, anxious, hesitant,* and *afraid*—in a confident, supportive tone that assures others you are not implying criticism. A patronizing inflection to the comment, "Those people were really scared by the reorganization," can easily make it sound like the fear was their fault. You would mistakenly send the message, "Those weaklings!" rather than "We ought to figure out a better way to do things around here."

Broaching the subject of fear informally also gives you a chance to monitor the responses you get in return. If people jump into the discussion freely, you are already miles ahead. If not, it could be simply that they have not thought about fear as a workplace issue. Keep up the informal comments and storytelling. Eventually, others will begin to add stories of their own.

If your introduction of the topic goes flat, it is possible that some of your own past behaviors as a manager are involved. Keep in mind that there is usually something about a manager's conduct and performance that has been intimidating to others. Suppose, for example, that you mention a fear-causing behavior such as making secretive decisions, and the room goes silent. People give each other meaningful glances but avoid eye contact with you. In the awkwardness of the moment, recognize that you have just stumbled across an important opportunity.

Make an observation to the group, such as "Looks like I've stepped into something pretty important," or "From the looks of your reaction, I suspect we could use some conversation around this one." People will probably laugh nervously after you make your observation. Then ask people to talk to you about why the room went silent. Tell them that this is *exactly* the kind of discussion that needs to take place before you can collectively move forward to reduce the amount of fear in the work environment. Then be quiet and listen to what people have to say.

Throughout your work with issues related to fear, accept the fact that you will probably discover things to improve personally, and it is vitally important that you model a positive response to getting feed-back. In this regard, you will probably find Chapter Eleven, "Value Criticism: Reward the Messenger," very helpful.

OVERCOME DENIAL

Another possibility is that the silence in the scenario just described means that people are in a state of denial. Denial is an instinctive retreat from something that is potentially threatening—very natural for a topic like fear. In addition to silence, denial is often characterized by many different types of objections from people. The following comments may be identified as signals of denial.

- When people do not see fear as part of their work environment or as applying to their organization and relationships, they may say:

    " I just don't see how this fear issue applies around here. It might be true for other people or someplace else, but I don't see how it fits the operations division. "

- When they do see fear, but as a human relations issue unrelated to the "real" work of the organization, you may hear:

    " I don't see why we should spend more time talking about this stuff. I just want to do my job. "

- When they are personally very confident and consider fear a sign of immaturity, inexperience, or personal weakness, comments may include:

    " It's not my problem if other people don't speak up. If some-body is too mealy-mouthed or insecure to talk about what's bothering them, then maybe they haven't got a point. "

- When they think of fear as an inevitable part of organizations, you may hear the expression:

    " Sure there's fear around here, and you're never going to get rid of it either. "

- When they don't see fear as having much of an impact on quality or productivity, or they think it increases them, a classic response is:

  66 *Frankly, a little fear isn't such a bad thing to keep people on their toes.* 99

- When they are concerned that they will have to make personal changes if this topic is "taken too far," worries may be voiced by saying:

  66 *This training is all well and good, but it doesn't apply to the real world.* 99

These variations of denial boil down to the feeling, "That's not us," or "That's not me." Of course, it is possible that fear is not a major issue in your organization, but we would guess that enough is present to warrant your consideration. Usually the objections are warning signals that something about the way the topic has been communicated does not allow people to make a personal connection comfortably. It would seem that addressing fear might lead to criticism or fault finding. We suspect that what often is in the way is the apparent negativity of fear as a topic. We learned this lesson the hard way as the following story reveals.

During part of our research effort we made a presentation to the management team of one of the participating companies. The team was made up of about 175 executives, managers, and supervisors and included the chairman of the board, the vice-chairman, and the CEO. Earlier in the day, we had been quite successful in reporting to a small group of top officers a summary of responses from a sample of previously interviewed company employees. We reported how the sample group's answers to the questions about undiscussables, reasons for not speaking up, and the impact of fear compared with results from our research effort as a whole.

At the evening presentation for the larger group of managers, we followed a nearly identical format. We included an opportunity for the managers, working in small groups, to briefly identify what they believed were the company's undiscussables. In a gratifying way the undiscussables surfaced by these table groups seemed to match the data we were about to report from the interviewed employees. Once those sample data had been presented by us and compared to the broader research findings, we turned to the whole group and asked the leading question, "Does this mirror your experience with this company? Do these data ring true?"

Loud shouts of "No way!" echoed across the room. We were shocked and a bit confused. "How come?" we asked the managers. Suddenly, we found ourselves answering lots of questions about how the sample of employees had been chosen, whether it reflected a vertical slice of the organization (it did), and whether it included enough people. We had a classic "that's not us" response on our hands. We forged ahead with the presentation, feeling as if we had endured a sufficient gash in our credibility for one day.

Ultimately the evening was saved by two events. First, the human resources director pointed out before our talk finished that we had omitted one vital piece of information used at the earlier presentation to officers. We had reported to the officers, but not the managers, that many of the employees interviewed commented on how much they liked working at the company. The second event was the commentary made by the CEO at the end of the presentation. He reminded his team that the glass at their company was more than half full. He then told them of his own experiences in getting personal feedback and the need to listen to the news, good or bad, about management conduct and performance.

This was a sharp lesson for us about flooding people with data that could be heard as critical of their organization or their own performance. The human resources director's reminder and the CEO's "more than half full" line go right to the core of the issue of denial. No matter how bad things might be, people want to feel good about themselves and their circumstances.

We next present suggestions to help you deal with denial in your organization.

Place the Topic of Fear in Context

In most organizations fear is part of the background, not the foreground. Remind people of the many things that are already going right and celebrate these things. Encourage people, however, to look for the "silent" organization, the opportunities that are lost because people hesitate to offer their ideas. This can be done in both formal and informal settings. Informally, you can weave these concepts, ideas, and questions into your interactions with most of the people you encounter. More formally, at large or small staff meetings, structured discussion questions using a brainstorming technique can be helpful:

❝ *What strengths do you see in our current operations?* **❞**

> " What barriers keep you from being as successful as you would like to be? "

> " Which of those barriers involve undiscussable issues? Fear of repercussions? A sense that things won't change? "

> " If this were an organization where people offered their ideas without hesitation, how would things be different? What kinds of things would we be doing? How would our customers be served differently? "

Take a "Systems Approach" to Fear, Rather Than Blaming People for Its Presence

Concentrate on the fact that fear is a heritage based on hierarchical systems and negative assumptions, not just temperament or the flaws of individuals. Use the cycle of mistrust as a catalyst for conversation. In one-on-one situations or small groups, engage people in discussions about the negative assumptions bosses make about employees and vice versa. Pose questions like the following ones:

> " Which of these negative assumptions do you see going on in our interactions? "

> " What kinds of self-protective behavior—on both sides—do the negative assumptions inspire? "

> " What's the gap between our intended behavior and how it is perceived by others? "

> " What can we do to turn this cycle around? "

While you lead discussions of this nature, be sure to be a participant as well. Describe how you feel about things. Let people know that you get frustrated and are sometimes tense or anxious. Make sure the tone in your voice is not interrogative. Your questions and manner should convey genuine interest and a desire for a mutual exchange of ideas. Save your perspectives until others have had a chance to share their points of view.

Take a Developmental Approach to Fear

No matter how good things are, they usually can be made even better. More than half full is great, but it is not the full glass. Reducing fear should be seen as a long-term enhancement, not a remedial fix. One method is to brainstorm with others the list of barriers that keep people from being as successful as they want to be. Pull out the items that are task focused and that could benefit from a rational problem-solving process. Initiate action on high-priority items. For those subjects that are more emotional or are tied to individual behavior patterns or group dynamics, take a more gradual, developmental approach.

Marvin Weisbord, in *Productive Workplaces,* offers sound advice:

> Any task, at some point, may shake people into Denial when the going gets rough. When that happens I don't know what to do except to keep talking and wait it out. . . . We are all subject to anxiety and craziness under stressful change. People need support to stay where they are a while longer under those conditions, not admonitions to hurry up and change faster [1987, p. 269].

These steps alone will not address all types of denial. Some individuals may want "proof" of fear's negative impact. Others may be convinced that it is too big or too entrenched in organizations to be turned around. Our advice is to accept these doubts and skeptical questions as legitimate, valuable counterpoints. Ask people to keep those questions handy and to watch for the evidence that answers their concerns. Do not exclude these perspectives. Rather ask that people think about and evaluate the information for themselves. Allow enough time for the ideas to percolate.

USE A CHECKLIST OF POSSIBLE SYMPTOMS AND COSTS OF FEAR

A checklist can be a helpful way for many people to begin understanding how fear affects the workplace. The following list of possible "symptoms" of fear is a good way to build awareness, particularly if you have encountered some elements of denial. There are three fundamental questions which individuals should answer for each item:

- Is it happening here?
- What might it have to do with fear, particularly the fear of speaking up?
- What costs—tangible or intangible—are associated with each item for employees, managers, and the organization?

The possible symptoms include:

- Lawsuits against the company
- Labor unrest, formation of unions, and hard bargaining; strikes
- Lack of suggestions for improvements and innovations
- Loss of customers who complain about poor service or products
- Turf battles over resources, assignments, and roles
- "Us versus them" talk
- Complaining after a meeting is over
- Unwillingness to take responsibility for mistakes; cover-ups
- An overly large number of personnel policies; an enforcement approach to rules; continuous arguments about the rules
- Many layers of approvals for simple decisions
- Many sequences of checking for simple transactions
- "CYA" activities
- People behaving politically
- Negative feelings about the company; lack of pride or commitment
- "Could care less" approach to the work
- Stressful work conditions or relationships
- Cynicism
- Bad decisions or indecision
- Grievances and employee complaints
- Resistance to performance appraisals
- People feeling that they get no feedback
- Expensive training programs aimed to "fix" employee or management performance
- Meetings where no one asks questions or no problems are solved
- Recurrent absenteeism and tardiness problems
- Missed schedules
- Instances of unethical behavior
- Financial or budget problems
- Continual EEO issues and harassment charges
- Resignation of high-quality performers and creative thinkers

- Eleventh-hour reports admitting that a project will not work
- Commitment to projects that people know are a waste of time and money
- A very active rumor mill
- Widespread dissatisfaction with promotions, assignments, and terminations
- Threatening behavior by supervisors, managers, or employees

Not every item on the list necessarily represents a sign that fear is alive and well in your workplace. Yet the list gives individuals something concrete against which to test their own experience. Discussing it can lead people to observe how easy it is to take fear and its costs for granted. As people share their perspectives, they may begin to see behavioral patterns in a new light, understanding the sometimes subtle way fear and mistrust influence daily activities.

SHARE YOUR CONCERNS WITH YOUR LEADERSHIP TEAM

As you proceed with building awareness, pay special attention to the feelings and experiences of the managers and supervisors who report to you. As you become more aware of fear, you may see elements of their behavior that you want to influence. In fact, sometimes interest in reducing fear starts from watching subordinate managers operate. However, nothing will kill your attempt to reduce fear faster than alienating these key players by creating a remedial program targeted to one or two people.

Mid-level managers and first-line supervisors often voice concerns about being caught in the middle. When the folks at the top get a new idea, these mid-level people are sometimes involved in the initial thinking and decision making. Frequently, they are not. Yet they are the individuals usually charged with implementing countless new programs and initiatives, many of which languish after a flurry of executive attention and the spending of much money. These requests come, of course, while they are also expected to maintain smooth daily operations. This double demand causes middle managers to become understandably skeptical about "another new management program." For these reasons, your interest in reducing fear by managing people in new ways is likely to trigger at least some hesitancy on their part.

Early on, bring the managers and supervisors who report to you into the circle of your concern and intentions. Ask for their help. Get *their* assessment of how fear affects the whole organization. Ask them how *they* want to proceed. Do this in small groups or in one-on-one discussions.

Initiate discussions in which you tackle the dilemmas of doing things differently. Give them a chance to raise concerns, some of which may be undiscussables. For example:

   66 *Human relations initiatives are all good and fine, but who will mind the store?* 99

   66 *Where will we get the time to manage this?* 99

   66 *What does this mean in terms of the expectations for our jobs? How do we need to behave differently?* 99

   66 *Does this new interest mean that you are dissatisfied with the way we have been doing things?* 99

People may assume that the concern with fear is simply one more fad. Until these underlying concerns are on the table and there has been a chance to address them, you should expect people to have a divided response. If you have more than one level of managers and supervisors reporting to you, give those at the higher levels a chance to think through these issues for themselves before their direct subordinates are involved.

In any such discussions, remember that these managers and supervisors may simply try to tell you what they think you want to hear. After all, you are the boss. Your approach should be easy and low-key, creating enough psychological safety so that people will be honest with you about what they *really* think of your plans to reduce fear.

MODEL WHAT YOU WANT

A market analyst for a corporation said it this way: "Most managers don't understand how damaging the gap is between words and actions and don't see the gap they create." In the effort to move forward and to create change, managers frequently trip over their own feet by not modeling what they want. Because of this, despite a world of good intentions, they do not get what they want. Unless you, as a manager, are willing to make some type of visible change in the way you manage and interact with others, those who report to you will not believe that you really want to reduce the amount of fear in your work environment.

We are reminded of one such data processing manager who was interested in creating a spirit of vitality in his team. He was mystified by the "somber" quality of his interactions with many of those who reported to him. Our encounters with him were universally positive and engaging. He expressed a strong commitment to creating a warm, supportive work environment for his employees. He impressed us as a classic "warm fuzzy" kind of manager, along with being an astute and efficient administrator.

It was not until we talked with some of his employees that we began to get the full picture. They said that they liked the manager as a person, but they wanted him to talk to them and involve them. One felt that she had "gotten off on the wrong foot" with him and said that it would be very difficult to fix the relationship now. She added that she wanted to be valued and appreciated. Another employee commented, "He doesn't pass the time of day with anybody in the office. He only talks to Debbie and John. He should just ask us out to lunch."

A third employee was concerned about recent changes in the corporation, including big issues of business direction. But she said that it was "hard to talk about heavy business philosophy when he doesn't greet you on the street." She went on to say that she felt he was "always physically walking backward out of his office" when she tried to talk to him and that she felt inadequate and incompetent in his presence. "I get panicky when I meet him the hallway," she added.

In addition to these signs of distance, there was a bigger issue in the background—his handling of a very abrasive supervisor who previously had made the lives of these employees miserable. It had taken several years for the abrasive boss to move into another capacity. One of the employees exclaimed, "Here's a manager who supported this abhorrent behavior—he allowed it to continue!" He had not talked to them about their feelings or the reasons the abrasive supervisor had been allowed to maintain her position. In the eyes of his subordinates, the manager left a wide gap between his intentions for a people-oriented workplace and the realities of his organization. No wonder there was tension in his relationships.

This vignette illustrates that to model what you want usually involves taking the risk of changing some aspect of your personal behavior. If you do not do so, others will not have a guide for their actions. The following suggestions will support this goal.

1. If you want people to disclose their fears, recognize and be able to talk about some of your own.

2. If you want people to speak up about sensitive issues, demonstrate that you can communicate about such issues. Perhaps more importantly, show that you are willing to listen to the concerns of others—even if what they present is difficult for you to hear.

3. If you want people to stop making negative assumptions, freeze those assumptions in yourself. Notice them as they come to mind and consciously bypass them in favor of a more constructive, accurate view of people and their motives.

4. If you want others to ask questions about fear's presence, be willing to ask those same questions first.

To illustrate the fourth point, we would like to return to the presentation we mentioned earlier in this chapter. During the evening, we saw the corporation's second highest officer do a simple thing. He turned to the person next to him at the dinner table, a customer relations supervisor many layers lower in the organization, and asked the question, "What do you think? Is there fear in this organization?" His tone was very natural and sincere. He was not at all defensive. He just wanted to know. She turned to him and said with equal naturalness and candor, "Of course." "Really?" he asked. "Oh sure," she replied. "It's all over the place. I see it every day." "You do?" he asked. "I'd really be interested in hearing about what you are seeing."

They spent the next few minutes in a very interesting conversation. He had modeled perfectly, and perhaps without really knowing it, the very first step someone in his position might take to acknowledge fear's presence.

10

PAY
ATTENTION
TO
INTERPERSONAL
CONDUCT

Once fear's presence and negative impact are acknowledged, managers can begin to think about steps to isolate and reduce it. We think that a solid first step is to help supervisors, managers, and executives avoid abrasive or abusive conduct. This is a good starting point for several reasons: (1) abrasive and abusive behaviors create immediate and direct repercussions for others; (2) the vast majority of those who hold leadership responsibilities already agree that these behaviors are unsatisfactory; and (3) in order to prevent problems, it is always helpful to know what *not* to do.

To begin this chapter, therefore, we present a fairly detailed description of abrasive and abusive managerial behaviors. If you see these behaviors in your organization—or yourself—this list may help you recognize them and begin to eliminate them. Later in the chapter, we will provide specific suggestions for intervening with and coaching others who exhibit this conduct.

Our proposals strongly emphasize the importance of first developing a shared vision of positive relationships and building awareness through education. For the vast majority of people, the objective is to define and make commitments to build supportive work relationships through positive norms. Tough interpersonal coaching, based upon a clearly delineated standard of conduct, may be required in some instances, but not many.

SHADES OF GRAY:
THE CONDUCT PEOPLE NEED TO AVOID

In Chapter Six, we reviewed a broad variety of managerial behaviors and organizational practices which frequently cause people to be afraid and presented a list specifically describing the abrasive behaviors to be avoided. That list—here referred to as a "gray scale" because it describes behaviors in order of their effects—is taken one step further in Figure 5. We have combined the gray scale with a second dimension for intensity to create a comprehensive model of the abrasive/abusive conduct sometimes displayed by people in management positions. It is important to note that employees and peers also can behave in these ways. But since we intend in this chapter to help managers exhibit respectful and trustworthy behavior, the model is presented from the perspective of what they may do to threaten those who report to them.

The gray scale and intensity dimension address the severity of impact in different ways:

1. The gray scale (numbers 1 to 11) describes the various types of behaviors. These are generally arranged in order of increasing

impact. For example, yelling and shouting typically have a more serious impact than simply being abrupt. We would describe as *abrasive* behaviors that are near the light-gray end; those at the dark-gray end are described as *abusive*.

2. The intensity dimension (letters A to E) places each fear-causing behavior on a continuum of subtlety, generality, frequency, and exposure. For example, there are many different ways insults and innuendos can be delivered. They may be more like an innuendo at point A, or they may happen infrequently. By comparison, at point E, the insults would come across as frequent, direct, and personal attacks made in a more public way. Because fear-causing behaviors are highly situational, we have not attempted to describe points A through E in detail. This intensity dimension is simply an aid to help you think about the wide variety of ways in which behaviors can be fear provoking.

The scales help to conceptualize the dynamics of abrasive and abusive conduct. A behavior which seems less threatening overall, such as abruptness, may still have greater impact if it is extreme or done

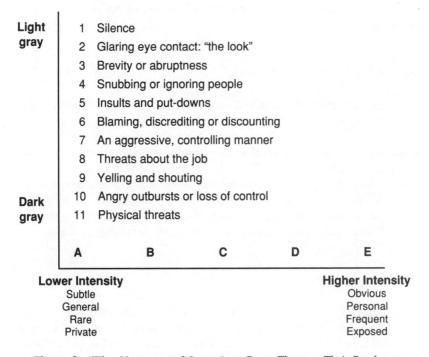

Figure 5. What Managers and Supervisors Do to Threaten Their Employees

in front of others. Similarly, an aggressive, controlling manner can come in a variety of amplitudes. Subtle, manipulative forms of aggression, if they are repeated frequently, can be very frightening. In other cases, a single instance—say a threat to someone's job in no uncertain terms—may have a dramatic, long-lasting impact.

These combinations and possibilities mean that fear is provoked in countless ways, and that any type of fear is a problem. Many of the behaviors on the gray scale have been identified in other research (Stringer, Pepitone-Arreola Rockwell, and Pearl, 1989). Here is a closer look at each one, with examples that primarily lean toward the extreme side (points D or E). As you read through the list consider the subtler side as well, drawing on your own experiences or those of others.

Silence

Silence can be a useful and appropriate tool to elicit communication from others. However, pausing and allowing the pause to continue, especially if it is accompanied by direct, deadpan, or cool eye contact, can be extremely intimidating. It is interpreted as questioning the speaker's judgment. People fumble inside trying to figure out what to say next.

Glaring Eye Contact: "The Look"

Some people can look at others with sufficient power to wither the brightest flowers of confidence. This is more than just eye contact. The look is a testing, evaluative glare. Vaguely irritated or on the verge of criticism, it is often filled with parental messages such as "What did you do this time?" or "You and I both know you are screwing up." It may also send the message that there is not much to hope for from the speaker: "What do you want now?" or "This better be good. I don't have much time." Combined with silence, the look is a powerful way to shut down communication—all without saying a word!

Brevity or Abruptness

This behavior is what one research participant described as "short, sharp answers" to questions or comments, using words that have a clipped, cold feel to them. "When I questioned a top decision," said one first-line supervisor, "my boss pointed his finger at me and shut me down. He snapped: 'It was a good decision.' That was the end of the conversation. There *was* no reason."

Snubbing or Ignoring People

This behavior separates people into castes: "I'm up here. You are down there." It can take the form of simply not talking to people, leaving them out of meetings important to their jobs, or reminding them of their "place." In response to a question from a clerical employee about a retreat for managers at an expensive resort, the top person's response was, "Other companies do it and it's none of your business." A manager described his observations of this phenomenon as "the male dominance ritual: put downs, in-crowd conversation, sitting in the power seats, turning one's back on someone at the meeting, stubbing out a cigarette in front of somebody at the table. In general, making sure everyone knows they are very, very important."

Insults and Put-Downs

These represent the commonly cited fear-provoking interpersonal behaviors: cutting remarks, direct or implied, that attack a person's credibility, self-esteem, or integrity. They often take the form of labeling, making jokes at someone's expense, ridicule or sarcasm, and racist, sexist, and other discriminatory remarks of all kinds. The impact of these comments is a combination of both fear and anger, permanently engraving the remarks in people's memories. Stories are numerous:

- A supervisor told one of his employees, "You're not as good as the other clerk. You don't understand computers; you don't have a mind for math."

- A senior manager for a service organization of 2,000 people was subject to his boss's abrasive commentary: "You are as important as the hole left in water after you pull your hand out." Apparently, this was a typical comment for this boss. He was known for a highly parental approach, even though his subordinates were the same age as he was. The senior manager recounted an incident in which "he took me by the arm and pulled me into his office with the phrase,'Step into my office, son.'" The manager described the boss as "pursing his lips, sitting up in his seat, and looking down at me like a child. 'This is just like raising children,' he said."

- In another situation a supervisor became irritated when her phone line kept buzzing. "Who's the idiot who's ringing my line?" she snapped. The employee who was in charge of the phones told the boss that she wasn't doing it. "No?" loudly replied the boss, "Then who is the *other* idiot?"

These are not just instances of people having a bad day. This type of behavior was described as a habit by employees, something that happened routinely. We were impressed with the clarity with which people recalled these events. A single remark would go a long way and last a long time.

Blaming, Discrediting, or Discounting

These behaviors place responsibility for the problem on someone else. The process is one of labeling or fixing blame in a way that traps or targets the other person.

In an earlier example from our interviews we told the story of a woman who had gone to the CEO to complain about her supervisor's abrasive behavior. She reported to us that the CEO had dismissed the situation as a "woman versus woman" conflict. In another situation, an office coordinator discussed morale problems caused by a co-worker with the co-worker's boss. She reported that her discussion resulted in her being blamed for the problem. The manager was a " 'finger pointer'—you really had to document things up to your neck. He'll twist things, dump blame on people. You really have to cover your behind."

In a third scenario, a change in management led to major personnel changes. When an employee, a buyer for the company, received her performance evaluation, she found that she had been criticized for her "lack of organization and follow-through"—areas that she said were actually her strengths. At a later meeting one of the managers made the public comment, "We are not going to be promoting any more secretaries to buyer around here." She was the only secretary in the company who had been promoted in this way. These discrediting remarks about her performance preceded her transfer to another part of the organization and eventual layoff.

An Aggressive, Controlling Manner

People described this autocratic behavior as demanding, intense, "my way or the highway." A secretary reported that the head of the operation called looking for her boss. She explained that he was at the barbershop. "Barbershop!" he exclaimed. "What barbershop? Go find him. Get him to me." In another case, a boss was described as "banging her fist on the table. She wanted people jumping and under pressure." This type of behavior easily blends with a micro-managing, high-surveillance approach to controlling people, such as requiring time logs for every task.

Sometimes this behavior is calculated and manipulative. It is at this point on our behavior scale that abrasive behavior can become abusive. A high-level program manager described working for a vice-president with a reputation for yelling at people. The manager reported that the first time this happened to him, he confronted his boss. "I told him he wouldn't treat me that way in the future. He smiled at me when I got done, and he never yelled at me again." His story continues:

> 66 Not long after that confrontation, I was in a meeting with him and some of his chief managers. He publicly dressed one of them down—up one side and down the other. And then he did something that told me it was all an act—it was just for the pleasure of exercising his power. In the middle of yelling at this guy in front of the others, he turned to me and winked. 99

Threats About the Job

Comments like "I'll remember this. You are undermining me," and "I can replace you" put the employee's job security on the line. Threats can be either implied or direct. Performance criticisms related to a particular project can include an unstated threat of job loss. When the boss says, "I'll get somebody else," as one top manager heard, it raises the question "for what?" A variation is to make the threat public. A market analyst reported an angry office scene in which a higher-level manager threatened to terminate the analyst's boss. "I'm going to fire you!" he shouted. After that the analyst reported that he "was shaking." He and others were "not willing to share true feelings or opinions. We were all waiting for management direction. It made us slaves. We felt we were not free to make statements. We really had no power or say."

Yelling and Shouting

Next to put-downs and insults this category, the loud voice or loud argument, was the most frequently cited interpersonal behavior that causes fear. Sometimes, people said, someone's voice was loud enough to be heard "all the way down the hall" or "all over the building," as if the venting was intended to widely publicize a failure and to humiliate the employee. One person commented that her boss seemed to "like the adrenaline rush" of loud arguments. A supervisor remembers hearing his boss say during one of these sessions, "Bob's been pouncing on me, so now you are going to get it, too." It is not unusual for obscenities, threats, and insults to be thrown into the bargain.

Angry Outbursts or Loss of Control

This behavior represents an explosion. It is the point at which people throw things in their offices or resort to exaggerations. For example, a group of employees tried to give their supervisor feedback about her style. As the group talked to her, she started to cry and turned their statements around. She accused the team of "ruining her career" and going to her boss behind her back. She threatened to hold them "directly responsible." In another company, the CEO had a reputation for blowing his stack. He would get so angry that his pant legs would hike up. There was an underground rating system among the managers about whether a particular episode was a "one-leg" or "two-leg" tantrum.

Physical Threats

Physical threats are only one step away from patently criminal behavior. In the following story, the threat is not spoken but it is surely felt.

> 66 I did not think my boss was technically competent. Our conversations would get adamant and personal. He would twist my words, so that I felt 'damned if I did and damned if I didn't.' I did a lot of rear-end covering. All our conversations degenerated into him yelling at me and my leaving. He violated my personal space, and I felt trapped and became afraid he would assault me.

> 66 At the end of one workday after many others had left, he followed me into my cubicle. He whispered harshly, 'You will do this!' I backed up to a corner. His fists were clenching and unclenching. He was breathing rapidly and his shoulders were heaving up and down. He had a wild look in his eyes. I thought he was going to hit me. At that point my values kicked in.

'You're harassing me,' I said to him. My boss defused at that point and walked away. Nobody was there to help.

❝ *I fell apart. It was hell. I went home and called the employee relations rep. I was afraid to go back to work. As far as I know, he was never reprimanded. He wasn't fired. I had a real fear for a long time afterward about working at night. It was a feeling of terror.* **❞**

ESTABLISHING POSITIVE GROUP NORMS

As we mentioned at the beginning of this chapter, eliminating the negative behaviors we have just described is primarily an educational and awareness-building process. A low-key way to begin that process with subordinate managers and supervisors is to develop a common picture of the positive relationships you and they naturally want to maintain with employees. This picture, without overly emphasizing negative conduct, then becomes a set of ground rules or norms for future behavior. Effective norms are created and agreed to by the group itself. They are oriented toward understanding, awareness, and the development of people, not enforcement of rules.

Develop a Picture of Positive Relations by Involving People in a Norm-Setting Discussion

For example, a division head might engage the managers who report to her with questions such as "What are the characteristics we would most like to achieve in our relationships with those we supervise?" or "What behaviors should we as individuals strive for in order to maintain quality relationships with employees?" Some of the material in Chapter Eight, "Build Relationships Without Fear," may be a good catalyst for such discussions. An excellent time to hold this type of discussion is in conjunction with work events that naturally lead toward planning and reflection, such as when the group

- Starts on a major new project or change effort
- Evaluates its progress over the last year
- Discusses its mission, goals, and objectives
- Returns from an important management training session

- Evaluates the organization's performance appraisal process or practices
- Addresses human resources issues, such as employee development programs

Guidelines such as the following ones may come from these discussions and then become the group's norms:

- Listen to employees; take time to hear their concerns.
- Give employees the benefit of the doubt—if things seem to be going wrong, check out the situation before making negative assumptions; avoid labeling.
- Follow through on agreements; if you promise to do something, do it.
- Congratulate people on their successes, even the small ones.
- Look for ways to build bridges rather than walls.
- Don't always stay in your office; do some managing by walking around.
- Help people grow in their jobs.

Record the Ideas from This Discussion and Distribute Them to Members of the Group

Norms can become a kind of measurement tool, enabling people to notice behavior and take action if it strays from the agreement. The commitment members of the group make to help one another act according to these norms is a very important part of the process. In addition to generating a positive picture, the group needs to answer such questions as

- What are our agreements about giving one another feedback on behaviors that do not match the norms?
- How will we measure progress toward meeting these norms as part of day-to-day interactions?
- What barriers do we foresee in meeting them and how will we overcome them?
- When will we next "check in" to assess our successes and potential areas for improvement?

Describe and Discuss the Gray Scale of Abrasive and Abusive Behavior

In a norm-setting discussion, the scale can help people generate positive behaviors. For example, if snubbing people is an example of abrasive behavior, what is its opposite? What are members of the group trying to achieve—a sense of equity? involvement? accessibility? Sometimes working from the bad example helps individuals identify the positive alternative. If the gray scale is used in this way, be sure people understand that you are using it as an informational resource, not as an indirect means to critique the group or individual members. Leaving this impression could hurt the credibility of the process and undermine commitment to its outcome.

With sufficient trust, members of the group may wish to volunteer some of their own experiences. If someone does so, have the person try to clearly identify the behavior that was a problem and place it in the model in terms of behavior type and intensity. These examples will help people understand dynamics such as subtlety, frequency, and circumstance.

USING THE GRAY SCALE TO ESTABLISH A STANDARD

If you find that positive norm setting is insufficient to deal with patterns of abrasive behavior on the part of those who report to you, consider using the gray scale more directly. In this case, the scale really does become a standard which you expect people to achieve. While the process for developing a standard is not markedly different from that used to create norms, your leadership role will shift. You will need to be more precise regarding your intention to hold people accountable for following the standard.

Use the Behavior Scale to Increase Awareness of Threatening Behaviors

In one-on-one situations or group meetings with your subordinates who supervise others, raise your concern about the behavior scale. Using our format as a model, involve people in a discussion about their views of threatening behaviors. Ask them to identify examples of our scale or suggest that they create a scale of their own, based upon their own experience and observation. Report some of your personal observations about behaviors in the group without targeting or embarrassing individuals. Reflect together about situations in which any of you might be inclined to exhibit some of these behaviors. Encourage an exchange of ideas and feedback with such lead-ins as

    66 *Let's talk about the things that punch our hot buttons, causing us to behave in ways we don't like.* 99

    66 *Which of these behaviors are any of us most inclined to use? Under what circumstances?* 99

    66 *What impact have we seen as a result?* 99

    66 *Which of these behaviors is the most offensive to any of us— when it is done to us? Why?* 99

    66 *Tell me, which of these do you see me doing? How are you affected when I behave this way?* 99

    66 *How important is it to you that we work together to eliminate these behaviors?* 99

Develop a Standard for Your Work Area

Once awareness has been raised, help people collaborate on a code of conduct for the group. Depending on the amount of fear you sense in the line that reports to you, you can approach this task formally or in a more casual way. The less formal approach can take place in a simple continuation of the discussion described in the previous section. Say something like

    66 *It sounds like we are all saying the same thing . . . that we want to become more conscious of the ways we might intimidate those who report to us. Can we simply agree that we are not going to do any of the things we've got listed here?* 99

Assuming that you get a positive response, carry the discussion one step further, as with the discussion of norms, and ask people: "How can we help each other live by this standard?" Spend some time talking about and making commitments to give each other feedback when you see or hear each other slipping into the gray scale.

If you and your subordinates decide that the presence of fear is significant enough for you to want to take a more formal approach, we suggest the following:

- Write down the behaviors you intend to avoid.

- Consider publishing your standard so that your employees will know what to expect from anyone who is in a supervisory position.

- Along with your direct subordinates, meet with employees to describe the standard in more detail and explain why it is being introduced.

- Schedule discussions at regular intervals to talk about progress or backsliding.

- For those who need assistance, yourself included, apply some of the ideas we present in the next section on coaching.

In the discussion and development of a standard, two events are likely to happen. First, people probably will not want to limit the standard to the negative aspects. They will want to include agreements concerning positive behaviors as well as the things they intend to avoid. By all means, make note of the positive commitments in the same way you would for the negative ones.

Second, the scale raises questions about people's impact on others and about perception, so you may hear "yes-buts" that relate to the need for the standard or the difficulty of living by it. You might hear the following comments:

> 66 But how do we avoid certain types of eye contact or jokes in this work group? I'm so used to relating to them in these ways that I'm not sure if I'll know when I'm doing anything I shouldn't. 99

> 66 What about employees who might be out to get one of us and who might accuse us of threatening them when it isn't true? 99

> 66 Why do we need to even be talking about this? It's only common sense not to do these things. 99

These concerns are reasonable but should not control the results. To reduce these concerns:

1. Listen carefully. Paraphrase points to demonstrate that you have heard what they have said.

2. Remind people that the list, as a standard, has two purposes: to make sure everyone knows what not to do and to reassure employees that you want to build an organization where people can speak up. If an employee does feel that a manager's jokes are causing anxiety, the scale may help that person to say so.

3. Remind people of the goal of this strategy—to talk openly about behavior, to clear up misperceptions, to get feedback, and to make changes if necessary.

4. Point out that the behavior scale really represents an assault on the cycle of mistrust. Some supervisors and managers may continue to worry about being blamed for things which are really not their fault. This is also evidence of the cycle at work.

COACHING SUBORDINATE LEADERS

Equal in importance to establishing norms and standards is giving and receiving feedback. When you see others exhibiting threatening behaviors—or the opposite behaviors which bring trust and support to relationships—you have an opportunity to intervene and to reinforce the goal of positive communications. The norms and standards that you and your team have developed, as well as the gray scale, provide a framework within which you can pass along your observations, accolades, and counsel and ask for feedback on your own behavior.

At its best this feedback process emerges naturally from the norm-setting or standard-setting work the group has accomplished. As people become more comfortable with the concepts and goals of improved interpersonal behavior, giving and receiving feedback become less tense and formal. They become part of the enjoyment of effective working relationships. Feedback at this level is in the vein of "observations" easily shared with others in the course of daily interactions. A conversation might go as follows:

| Manager | *66 I am wondering how Lori felt at the staff meeting this morning. She didn't say much, and I don't think either of us did much to draw out her ideas. Theresa, I think you and I spent a lot of time talking at the staff meeting, rather than letting employees share their ideas. 99* |

Assistant manager	**"** *I agree. Perhaps Lori is just feeling overwhelmed. It's hard to be new. We didn't ask questions, just talked about our projects.* **"**
Manager	**"** *I'm not sure how I'd feel right now if I were in her shoes.* **"**
Assistant manager	**"** *I'll check to make sure she's okay.* **"**

In addition to providing feedback directly, you can encourage those who report to you to gather information from other logical sources:

1. Suggest that each of your subordinate managers have those who report to them review the norms, standards, and gray scale and give them feedback directly. With sufficient support and training, this process could be continued throughout the whole organization.

2. Ask members of your team to make a targeted, personal assessment of their behaviors and yours. With sufficient trust, this might also be an excellent place for peers to give each other some feedback as well.

The most sensitive feedback, of course, is likely to be found in working with a subordinate supervisor or manager who has an ongoing pattern of abrasive or abusive behavior. Such subordinates can offer a particularly tricky challenge for their bosses and mentors. The employee may not even see the behavior, let alone view it as a problem. He or she may never have received feedback on personal conduct. Previous managers may have accepted it as simply part of the individual's style, especially if the person is a technical whiz. In situations like this, you are dealing with the individual's image of who he or she is at work. That concept is not an easy one to change.

Stowell and Starcevich (1987) in their work on coaching employees point out that most people know beforehand that a problem exists. Typically they do not change because they do not see the impact of the problem. In addition to simply stating that a pattern of abrasive or abusive behavior is unacceptable, the leader's role is to help the person recognize vividly how this pattern negatively affects others, the work, and the organization. Stowell and Starcevich point out that this is usually best done by asking good questions and providing good examples. Possibilities include:

" *Nguyen, if that same comment had been made about you, how would you respond?* **"**

“ *Ted, I've heard from some of your people that you can be really sarcastic at times: having an edge in your voice, using double meanings to make your point. These things always make someone feel uncomfortable. I know your job can be very frustrating. But I wonder if you have really evaluated the effects of this behavior. How do you think this type of thing is interpreted by your employees? What kind of impact do you think it has on the work?* ”

“ *Marcia, I've heard it said that you intimidate people with your communication style. It's in the look of impatience you give people sometimes and the abrupt tone in your voice. I know these may seem like small behaviors, but they are having a significant impact. I believe you are leaving the impression that your employees aren't any good at their jobs and should be scared of you. Is that what you mean to convey?* ”

“ *Javier, when you break a pencil to make a point about how upset you are, people focus on how they are being treated, not the message you are trying to send. What would you think if someone did that to you?* ”

“ *Susan, I could hear you shouting on the other side of the office. Do you know what that did to the staff? People stopped doing anything for at least an hour. All people did was talk and wonder who was getting it this time. My bet is that they will remember this incident for a long time.* ”

In each case, focus on describing concrete behaviors: what the person specifically has done or said that has created problems. If possible, describe the specific incidents and the pattern of behavior which has emerged. Then describe the nature of the consequences in each case. Listen to the employee's explanations carefully for clues as to why these behaviors are occurring. Then work together to establish more productive alternatives.

Suppose that a subordinate supervisor becomes abrupt and judgmental when she feels her authority has been challenged. Help the person name the emotions that lead to negative interactions. Perhaps her own sense that she is becoming defensive or confrontational can be a reminder for her to get away from the situation for a while or seek you out for counsel. Perhaps she's feeling, "I've earned my stripes. I shouldn't have to deal with this!" or "I have my rights!" Work in a collaborative way to get these emotions out in the open and then develop a plan to move past them with constructive behavior. Give the supervisor a chance to share the problem rather than face it alone.

Besides these direct feedback comments, there are other things you can do to assist your subordinate. For example:

1. Suggest customers and family members as likely additional sources of feedback.

2. Offer the individual the time and money to attend a seminar for developing communication and other positive interpersonal skills. Do not characterize this training as "charm school." Rather, actually go through the seminar with the person and compare notes during and after you attend. Your willingness to share the commitment to the training and your ability to use its vocabulary later will enhance the individual's chances for success.

3. Ask the person to assess his or her past experiences for events that seem to trigger abrasive or abusive conduct. Have the subordinate identify patterns and develop action plans to freeze the negative behavior before it happens.

Finally, our best general advice on coaching your subordinate managers and supervisors is to sit on the same side of the table. Nobody wants to be isolated with a problem. Talking about your own past experiences, gaffes, and blunders will help build trust. Make your coaching a mutual learning effort. The feedback you provide may have a distinct impact on your employee's insight and confidence.

Therefore, along with your constructive suggestions, comment on his or her special skills, talents, and accomplishments. Take a gentle, supportive approach but be persistent in your requirement for change. Forgive mistakes, but find time to talk about them. Do not let opportunities for learning go to waste. You must follow through.

These discussions may lead to feedback from your employee about your own leadership style. Discovering how he or she sees you can provide a rich opportunity to explore the nuances of your own interpersonal relations and to tear down a fence or two along the way.

WORKING WITH RESISTANT SUBORDINATE LEADERS

Most would agree that the hardest part of managing people is dealing with subordinates who do not meet performance expectations. This is especially difficult and frustrating after great efforts have been made to clarify the expectations, provide ongoing performance feedback, and arrange for coaching and other resources to help the person improve. This chapter would not be complete if we did not offer some suggestions about what to do when you decide that one of your subordinates is unwilling or unable to change and continues to do things which threaten others.

Two points are worth mentioning to begin with: If you really want to create a quality organization, certain behaviors must stop. There is a time and a place for establishing requirements, not just goals. Additionally, despite the confidential settings in which you will be working with your reluctant subordinates, it is good to keep in mind the phrase: "The whole world is watching." How you treat people who do not match the standard will probably be considered by others in the organization the greatest test of your ability to match your actions to your words. You must deal with obvious interpersonal problems if you want to maintain credibility as a leader.

If someone on your team takes action which upon investigation is found to be intentionally retaliatory, make your intervention swift and strong. This does not mean that it should be demeaning, but that it should be direct and to the point.

1. Ask the individual to reevaluate personal behavior in depth, including motives, interests, and style, comparing this behavior to the needs and standards of the organization.

2. Depending on the severity of an incident or pattern, you may wish to ask the individual to participate constructively or resign. *Participate constructively* means that the person eliminates abrasive and abusive behavior. Let the person know that if the pattern continues, you will have to make a choice about his or her continued employment with the organization.

3. If an individual acknowledges that his or her personal style is abrasive or abusive but openly states an unwillingness to change, you ultimately may have no choice but to proceed with a termination action. Before you do, be sure the employee has thought through his or her statements and their consequences.

With individuals whose actions look intimidating but who deny any retaliatory motive, be clear what the standards are and hold the individuals increasingly accountable for their actions.

1. Begin with a warning about what the situation looks like to you and to others. Reassure the person of your commitment to a fair and complete investigation of events. Assure him or her that you are not in the business of setting people up to fail. Then jointly

analyze the situation in question, and perhaps other past incidents, to show why the behavior seems retaliatory.

2. Ask the person to clarify for you and, more importantly, for his or her employees how these events were not punishments. This may require you to meet with your employee's subordinates in order to find out how these messages are actually heard. Are they believable? Why or why not? Be public about your desire to create a positive work environment and support for your direct subordinate's efforts to eradicate negative perceptions.

3. Consider using the services of a third-party consultant to facilitate discussions where your subordinate manager and his or her employees can safely exchange feedback. This outsider can also serve as an objective observer, providing neutral information about the behavior of the subordinate manager and the group.

If change does not occur as a result of these steps, you may be able to restructure the employee's position to a nonsupervisory role. Or you may decide to ask the person to reconsider his or her employment in the organization. Restructuring can be very sensitive. It should be done in a way that enables the person to genuinely learn from the experience without undermining self-esteem. Human resources professionals are often an important support for managers facing such situations.

The last scenario is working with someone who cannot change an abrasive or abusive style but who is sincerely trying to do so. This individual deserves respect, care, and attention.

1. Provide a referral to a helping agency or employee assistance program.

2. Help to arrange a mentoring relationship with another experienced manager.

3. Consider restructuring the position to one that does not involve supervision.

4. If problems persist, face up to it, and help your subordinate manager do the same. Be truthful and supportive. Engage the services of a competent outplacement counseling service or career development firm to help the individual become successfully reestablished in new employment.

In all of these difficult leadership situations, do your best to maintain a nonjudgmental role. There should be nothing vindictive or angry about your approach. All of these scenarios are a matter of placement:

the proper match between a person and a job, a role, or an organization. Do your best to accept with patience and forbearance this most challenging aspect of implementing a standard for interpersonal relations.

A final point to remember is that whenever a termination occurs, others may be scared. People close to the individual who has left the organization will probably have strong feelings about the situation. Without violating the dictates of conscience or advice of legal counsel, talk to your other employees about this event. Give them a chance to express their feelings and concerns. Describe, if only in general terms, the efforts that were made to correct the problem before the termination occurred. This can be a vital debriefing that puts the matter to rest.

FOSTERING ORGANIZATIONAL COMMITMENT TO POSITIVE INTERPERSONAL BEHAVIOR

Our strategies in this chapter have focused on a single manager and the people who report to her or him. We believe that there are no substitutes for trust and clarity in these relationships. There are, however, other actions which could support positive interpersonal behavior at a broader organizational level.

As a customer of your organization's training function, you may want to encourage consideration of a module on reducing threatening behaviors. The gray scale of behaviors might be usefully built into an organization's regular supervisory and management development efforts. Training programs are an excellent place—often because they are safer—to talk through and practice positive interpersonal skills.

Also, you may wish to talk with your own peers or supervisor about broadening the effort to improve interpersonal relationships throughout the organization. As an "insider," your skill in explaining how abrasive or abusive conduct undermines known business goals may help get that ball rolling. Be prepared to explain how negative conduct can have a major impact on quality and productivity. Advocacy and support from people inside the organization comprise an essential ingredient of change.

In the long haul, we believe that attention to interpersonal conduct is infectious. People become proud of their ability to improve communication with one another and become increasingly interested in the skills required to do so. Establishing positive norms and standards, education about behaviors to avoid, and day-to-day feedback gives direction and energy to working relationships. These steps overturn negative practices and feelings and directly address the behaviors that are most likely to cause fear.

11

VALUE CRITICISM: REWARD THE MESSENGER

The phrase "shoot the messenger" is a cultural and historical symbol for what happens to people who speak up. In three words, the implication is clear: "If I bring bad news, I will suffer for it." In this chapter, we describe why messengers are shot and provide recommendations to overcome this pattern. These include ways to hear and seek bad news and reward the messenger.

WHY AND HOW THE MESSENGER GETS SHOT

Messengers usually point out problems with people or systems—the messy situations that seldom have a simple answer or a quick fix. Those who hear bad news and shut off discussion may do so because they do not, in fact, know how to solve the problem. They worry, along with the messenger, that if the problem comes to light "I'll get in trouble" or "People will think I can't handle it." As one middle manager for a public agency commented, the "shoot the messenger" syndrome "comes from managers' fears of looking bad in front of their bosses. They all want to look like they are doing a good job." Plans, pet projects, and assumed understandings are shown to have flaws, gaps, and glitches. Such a message is one no one wants to hear when he or she is under the stress of the daily work load. It is easy to see why messengers become the targets when a manager's pride and commitments are at stake.

Messengers also get shot because their listeners make negative assumptions about their motives. It is easy to imagine that the messenger is doing something other than simply bringing news. A retired manager we spoke with asked us, "Don't you think these fellows who show up on your doorstep usually have a grudge of their own they are trying to work out?" Discounting the messenger in this way is self-protective. It is a sign of a negative assumption about the messenger's ill-will. When people "show up on the doorstep," the self-protective manager first wants to know what axe the messenger has to grind. The message gets lost as the cycle of mistrust invades with an evaluation of motives.

To change the perception that messengers ultimately cause harm requires commitment to the larger picture and a willingness to take risks. What is necessary is an attitude, personally and throughout the organization, that problems are prized possessions—learning opportunities which are essential to continued improvement and innovation. It takes recognition that the messengers do not *create* the problems; they simply help to *identify* them. Along with their other activities, people at all levels should be encouraged to spend time both locating trouble and discarding the blame.

Establishing a sense of personal trust is essential if you want people to speak up. If, as a manager, you have a reputation for genuinely wanting criticisms and handling them in a responsible, nondefensive way, people will talk to you. They will do so even if they do not know you personally or report directly to you. There is an obvious need in this trust-building effort to avoid behavior others see as repercussions. The steps we suggest in the following pages describe some specific ways to establish such a reputation.

HEARING THE BAD NEWS

We have often heard from clients that bad news may be hard to accept because of the way it is brought forward. The messenger's manner may be a disaster. The person may be blunt, accusatory, frustrated, and argumentative. There may be a raft of negative assumptions about your behavior and motives that underlie the person's conduct and that feel like an attack on your integrity. In addition, the messenger may have a history. He may, for example, be a vocal member of the union executive committee. His own performance may leave a lot to be desired. Perhaps he is skating by on a marginal attendance record.

Now, suddenly, he is in your office complaining about how a co-worker has been mistreated by her supervisor. Neither he nor his co-worker has talked to the supervisor directly and the complaint seems altogether minor. You find yourself wanting to snarl: "It's none of your blankety-blank business. Get back to work!"

Stop. Take a breath. Think for a moment. Do not expect the bad news to come to you in a palatable way. What you have in front of you is the minor concern of a highly resistant employee whose values and approaches long ago took on the colors of the cycle of mistrust. This is most likely the tip of an iceberg.

Do Not React Defensively

Keep in mind that the issue is not *how* the message first arrives, but *what* the message is. If you worry too much about their manner, you throw chairs in the path of people who already are nervous that coming to you will cause them to be seen as troublemakers. Requiring that people always be 100 percent polite, be constructive, and have solutions—not just problems—is a great way to narrow the number of individuals who will ever come to you. Such expectations will almost guarantee that when somebody does show up, that person will be angry, frustrated, and outspoken or, at the other end of the spectrum, will be indirect.

In this case, manner is a red flag signaling possible negative assumptions in your work force. If this person is in your office complaining about a minor issue, how many others in your group feel the same way? How deeply entrenched is the cycle of mistrust in your organization? If you find yourself privately complaining about "that damned union" or "those rotten apples," you are buying into the cycle and may be contributing to the problem.

Hear Out the Messenger's Full Message

Ask the messenger what else in the organization is going on, how people feel about working for you and others in supervisory roles, and what their range of concerns is. Once everything is on the table, you may find there is quite a bit of work for you to do. That's okay. Now you have a basis for further investigation and contact with people. You know that much more feedback and information is required. By listening carefully to this "troublemaker and boat rocker" you have heard the news, not only about a problem between an employee and a supervisor, but about your organization as a whole.

One of the reasons a messenger's style may be offensive is that he or she might be tense about approaching you, the subject of the conversation, or both. When people are uptight they do not express themselves as well as they might. In addition to having a nervous tone of voice, they may stumble over their words and ideas. They may be unclear, exaggerate, present inappropriately rosy or negative opinions, overly simplify things, or make them too complex. The best solution is to bring down the tension level so that the messenger can say what he or she really means.

Create a Comfort Zone

This is more complicated than offering a comfortable chair and a cup of coffee, although those things sometimes do help. It is much more a matter of tone, openness, and a willingness to slow down and listen to people. Even if the other side seems hostile, say things like

> 66 Okay, this sounds like it's pretty sensitive and important. Let's start at the beginning. 99

> 66 I'd like to get a sense of the full situation and how you and others are feeling about it. 99

❝ *I'm here to listen. I appreciate your views on this problem and I'd like to know why you personally think we've got it.* **❞**

Phrases like these defuse the tension by saying that you are open and accessible, and that you care about the other person's feelings and perspective. They are a mark of respect. They are, in the terms of conflict experts Roger Fisher and Scott Brown (1988, p. 37) an "unconditionally constructive" approach to others. They may also have the effect of bringing down your own tension level by killing the impulse to evaluate and defend, and replacing it with a desire for more information. Keep in mind the phrase: "Better to hear it now than later."

Search with the Messenger for the Systems Issues Behind the Scenes

The messenger can be as guilty of blaming people as anybody else. The problem may be stated as "that manager" or "that customer." The behavior of those parties may well be involved. But the bigger picture is that the problems brought by the messenger also may have to do with work systems, roles, policies, organizational structures, ambiguities of all kinds, or other problems that have little to do with conduct.

This search takes the conversation away from a hunt for the guilty, depersonalizes the problem, and aims the exchange toward a collaborative analysis of the business issues that need to be addressed. For example, someone complains to you about a manager's unrealistic performance expectations. It would be easy, given the cycle of mistrust, to get trapped into either arguing about whether they are or are not realistic or evaluating the motives behind the allegation. On the other hand, maybe there *is* something wrong with the way those expectations are being communicated. Perhaps a dispute between two senior managers, unclear decision-making roles, problems with the hiring process, or other issues are involved. Perhaps schedules are unrealistic. If so, what is causing *that?*

This is more than just a technique to get people to talk. Our interviews suggest that individuals' first concerns are personal, self-protective, and more oriented to the quality of work life than to suggestions for improving work. By helping move the conversation toward the larger issues, you encourage people to evaluate how their initial complaint relates to the systems by which the work gets done. This defuses tension and asks the messenger to become an active participant in the problem-solving process.

SEEKING BAD NEWS

Responding to the problems that come to you is a critical skill, but it is still a reactive one. To really open up communication requires more forthright action. You need to go out and find the problems. The phrase "If it ain't broke, don't fix it" leads to a certain degree of armchair confidence. It is as if you are saying, "If nobody is bringing me problems, I guess there aren't any." A different approach is to find out what condition the organization is really in.

There are a multitude of suggestions that could be offered as ways to seek information from employees. In the ones we emphasize, you communicate *in person* with those who work for you. Organizational assessments done by outside consultants, employee satisfaction surveys, employee task forces and standing committees, and electronic hotlines are other representative methods many organizations use very effectively. However, because reducing fear requires improving the manager-employee relationship, we call your attention to approaches that are targeted specifically toward enhancing those vital interpersonal interactions.

Ask Open-Ended Questions About the Work

At a basic level, this involves asking people directly for feedback on whatever is or might be a problem.

“ *How are things going?* ”

“ *What kind of problems are you running into?* ”

“ *If you were going to do this again, how would you improve it?* ”

“ *What barriers do you anticipate in the next phase of the work?* ”

“ *What are our customers saying about us these days?* ”

These questions can be directed toward work groups or individuals. Make an observation or share a related experience of your own to let people know that you sincerely want to know what is going on. Let people know why you want to know. Say clearly that you are interested in being of help and want to support their efforts. Listen carefully to their responses. Paraphrase what people tell you to make sure that you got their message.

Seeking the bad news means being more visible, participative, and openly receptive to information. This requires time and effort and a willingness to push yourself out of your daily routine to understand the routines of others. The following suggestion extends the concept of "management by walking around."

Take On an Actual Front-Line Role for a Day

Watch, learn, and ask questions about processes people use to produce a product or service. Get to know people, their names, what they do, and what they care about. Follow up with discussions with front-line and supervisory staff to identify problems and possible improvements.

One health-care administrator we know uses this technique on a regular basis. Once every two months, she makes sure that she is scheduled into one of the six outpatient clinics she oversees. There she assumes the role of the receptionist, working a full shift. She sees patients, their families, physicians, nurses, and technicians. And, perhaps more importantly, they see her working the front line, trying to understand their experience and the issues from their vantage point. This sends an important message about her respect for the work, the ideas, and the feelings of her employees.

Share with Others How Your Mistakes Have Been
Learning Opportunities

How you deal with your own mistakes also sends a message to others. Becoming defensive, covering them up, or seeing them as horrible faults will have the following results:

- People will worry that you will take bad news personally and might blame them for bringing it forward.

- You will teach your organization that mistakes should be handled personally and defensively.

- You will not hear about others' mistakes because they will worry about your negative reaction.

Show people you can forgive yourself and move on. Displaying your vulnerabilities in this way will make it easier for others to share their own fallibilities. In fact, telling a few selected stories about yourself—how you goofed, what you learned from it, how you did things differently the next time—does two things. First, it sends the message that it is okay to make mistakes. Everybody, including you, does. It makes you seem human to people who might have a tendency to put you on a pedestal or in a box. Second, it models your willingness to take responsibility for your own actions.

In *The Abilene Paradox,* Jerry Harvey writes, "When we make it difficult for organization members to acknowledge their mistakes and have them forgiven, we have designed organizations that reduce risk-taking, encourage lying, foment distrust, and, as a consequence, decrease productivity" (1988, p. 59). Harvey observes that a manager's ability to tell the simple truth and accept responsibility for a mistake is amazing to people who expect excuses or suggestions that others are really to blame. When managers tell the truth about themselves and their experiences, it comes as a breath of fresh air to those who expect anyone in a supervisory capacity to be distant and defensive. Such an act of self-disclosure "provides the basis for human connection. It relieves our alienation from one another" (p. 66). As a result, it makes it much easier for others to do the same.

Ask Your Team Directly for Feedback

Another important step in modeling the behavior you want is to ask your associates and subordinates to give you direct feedback on your performance and conduct. Our consulting experiences tell us that people who ask for feedback and create safe opportunities to receive it are truly playing out a leadership role. Asking for feedback gives you a better picture of the effects of your behavior on others. It will also reassure people of your intentions and accessibility in the long term. Use words such as these:

> 66 *Like most people, I am trying to make a conscious effort to improve my performance and my communication skills. I am not assuming that I am not successful, but there are a few things I'd like to get better at. What I am interested in is your feedback, positive and negative, about how you see me operating in my role. I'm not asking for anything fancy, and I certainly don't want B.S. I know people can be as reticent to give feedback as they sometimes are to receive it. But I would like to encourage you to be open. I want the good news and the bad, and I want to hear the truth.* 99

Depending on the nature of your team, you could follow up this statement by simply throwing the floor open for discussion. However, for all but highly interactive and trusting groups, that creates a fairly tough environment. There is a better route:

1. Request individual meetings to discuss your subordinates' perceptions. Ask the people who report to you to make a list in advance and to identify specific incidents that illustrate your positive traits and those you need to improve. Take a warm, natural approach to these meetings. Keep them private and uninterrupted. Be sure to ask people about the impact of the behaviors they identify on themselves and the organization.

2. Build a composite picture of how others view your leadership, both your strengths and areas needing improvement. When you finish with the meetings, identify a handful of patterns that have emerged. Report back to your team what you heard, and allow for some discussion and verification of your perceptions. Then communicate your plan to adjust your behavior and ask for the team's continuing support and feedback to you. For certain key concerns, you may want to seek ideas to pursue from the group.

3. If you sense that your employees would not respond comfortably to this level of direct feedback, bring in a consultant from outside your group. Have him or her interview your subordinates, synthesize their views, and present them to you—and them—in an aggregate, anonymous fashion. Collectively discuss the feedback and decide about future actions.

Remember that what you are doing is twofold. First, you are getting some information about yourself and your skills which can be vital to making personal improvements. Second, you are leading others to do the same thing. You are making it safe and encouraging people to get information as a part of their own personal growth and development. You are making the gift and acceptance of feedback part of the ethic of participation in your team.

REWARDING MESSENGERS

To fully turn around the "shoot the messenger" syndrome, managers need to make a conscious effort to reward people who speak up. The rewards we choose to highlight are not of a tangible nature. They emphasize appreciation for the openness and risk taking of the messenger. They demonstrate respect for the messenger's suggestions and observations through attentive follow-up action. They focus on building a constructive and ongoing relationship between you and the messenger. This will ensure your continued access to the information and insight of others.

Personally Thank People for Bringing Forward Their Concerns and Ideas

Acknowledge that speaking up is not always the easiest thing to do, particularly when it includes potential criticism or feedback on conduct. Tell what you will do, when you will do it, and when and how you will report about your progress. Let people know that their role as messengers is one that is vital to the continued success of the organization. Let them know that you *personally* appreciate the efforts that have been made.

Tell Natural Messengers How Much You Value Them

Some people naturally speak up no matter what the organizational environment. These are individuals who have not bought into the cycle of mistrust and who are naturally open with their feedback by virtue of temperament or experience. They are willing to raise issues and challenge conventional thinking. Ask them to help you out by keeping you informed about issues and concerns. Praise them when they bring you the news, good or bad. Consider their advice carefully, and act on their suggestions whenever it is feasible.

One executive we know relies on a director of research to bring him information about the organization and feedback on his management style. On more than one occasion, he has sincerely expressed his appreciation for her straightforward candor and commitment to communicating the bad news. Frequently, the research director has provided tactful, direct feedback regarding practical changes in the executive's interpersonal style that would make communication go more smoothly in the operational units. While acknowledging the importance of these ideas, the executive's actual behavior has remained essentially the same. This apparent reluctance to respond to the research director's messages has unfortunately given a frustrating double message to this loyal messenger and seriously eroded her trust in the executive. She has begun to wonder if it is worth the effort to keep bringing him feedback when she sees so little change.

Provide Concrete Examples of How Bad News Has Led to Improvements, Savings, or Innovations

Use hard data when possible, telling of production time cut, dollars saved, market share increased, customer complaints down, and compliments up. Celebrate and publicize this information.

Quality improvement efforts in an organization are often a rich source of stories that reinforce the value of bad news while praising the messengers. In one company, a staff department discovered that about 30 percent of its time was spent checking or correcting the work of others. The good news is that by evaluating several overly complex procedures, the department was able to reduce the amount of checking time significantly, along with reducing errors. The team saved about one-quarter of a staff analyst's time per year. Sharing information such as this is a way to promote the belief that bad news can be the catalyst for success.

Ensure Some Type of Response to Every Employee Suggestion

Along these same lines, it is essential that when suggestions are made by employees, you follow up on them. In Chapter Six, we described a variety of behaviors that cause fear. Failing to follow up on good-faith suggestions made by employees creates ambiguity and triggers, for many, anxious and fearful reactions.

Get back to people to let them know what is going to happen as a result of their suggestions. Typically, these include three options:

- You decide that follow-up is not necessary or possible at this time.

- You intend to get personally involved.

- You delegate the follow-up to someone else.

In each of these situations, thank the messenger for his or her efforts. As mentioned before, tell what you are inclined to do and give your reasoning. Be willing to discuss it if the messenger does not agree or understand your point of view. Be open to reconsidering your plan if new information surfaces during this exchange. If you delegate the response, describe what you will do to monitor the work someone else will do. When it is appropriate, create some type of involvement for the messenger. In one case this might be membership on a problem-solving task force. In another, it might mean that you will meet again in a month to discuss progress.

If, when you delegate a response, the follow-up does not occur as planned, investigate the situation. This may offer clues about communication and problem-solving barriers in your organization which need to be addressed.

Establish Response to Employee Ideas as a Priority for Your Subordinates

Talk about this issue at staff meetings; ensure that it is a routine part of supervisor and management training. In particular, remind people that when action has been taken, it is important to be sure that the messenger is informed about what happened. In cases where the messenger is part of the problem-solving plan, this will not be necessary. But in other situations, where the messenger expresses a concern and does not participate in the follow-up, he or she will not necessarily know that something has been done unless a conscious communication effort has been made. Some refer to this as *closing the loop*.

A front-line employee in a public agency talked to us about layoffs that had happened some years previously. The executive was criticized heavily by employees for the abrupt way in which these layoffs occurred. The employee we spoke with shared these concerns, but also commended him for the way he handled the bad news:

> 66 He asked us [the employee association] to meet with him. He didn't bury our memo criticizing the way he had handled the layoffs. He took action, setting up an employee task force to make recommendations for change. Then he acted on those recommendations. He went up in front of employees in the height of their anger. He took it all. I'll always respect him for that. 99

The executive did more. He continued to investigate the problems and brought in an outside consultant to assist him. This work led to several additional steps:

- Team development for senior levels of the organization
- Organization-wide training in communication

- The beginnings of a supervisory training program
- Revisions to policies that inhibited communication flow within the organization

A CASE IN POINT

Put together, these strategies create a strong statement of support for existing messengers and encouragement for new ones. In fact, the goal of the effort ought to be to make every person a messenger for the organization. A consulting story illustrates this point.

A marketing department director we worked with is an enthusiastic advocate of self-managing work teams. She passionately believes in pushing decision making down in the organization and has spent a lot of time and money on pilot projects and training to help managers and employees be effective in this new way of approaching work. Unfortunately, her personal style has been one that has confused people and caused them to hesitate to bring their concerns forward. When we first were asked to assist this person, both those who reported directly to her and employees farther down in the organization told us that they could not speak freely about the concept of self-managing work teams. They did not know what it really meant for them and their roles, but they felt that speaking up would be negatively interpreted as resistance by our client.

The department director was perceived to give mixed messages about involvement and openness. A noticeable proportion of her department believed that "no matter what she says, she doesn't walk the talk. So how can we trust her?" When things were not moving fast enough, she would get a sarcastic edge in her voice, rather than acknowledging, up front, her frustration and impatience. She was famous for her "look" that conveyed strong disapproval. When she would pose a question asking for input and no one would speak up, she would make the decision herself.

The director knew that things were not right but did not know what was going wrong. Fortunately, a few people within her department took the risk of talking about low morale and confusion about what "self-managing work teams really mean." With some help from us, the director sought feedback on the pilot projects as well as on her own personal style. When, at a recent staff meeting, her direct subordinates were teasing her about how "1989 will be remembered as the year Celia gave up 'the look,' " trust was obviously on the rise.

Being open to the messages about her personal communication style had other payoffs. Members of the group could express their confusion about the self-managing teams. Up to that point, there had been much suspicion and cynicism about "all the money that has been wasted on the self-managing work team pilots." These comments came primarily from people who had not been directly involved in the pilots, but who had heard stories about the "amount of time spent in meetings and away from the real work."

Opening up the discussion to consider this bad news led to a more systematic survey of how people who had been directly involved felt about the pilot projects. In fact, only one out of the fifty people involved said that he would not want to be part of a pilot project if he could do it again. This surprising result caused many to rethink their assumptions about the teams. Without the bad news having surfaced, the good news would never have been believed.

The door this leader opened was one to herself. She made a concerted attempt to model the willingness to seek feedback. In fact, she asked us, as consultants, to give her feedback on her management and communication style *in front of* her direct subordinates. We gave her that feedback honestly, and she used it as a catalyst for further input from those who reported to her. Near the close of the discussion, the director made clear her intention to change some of her unconscious yet intimidating behaviors. She said that she hoped, and expected, her managers to give her ongoing feedback in the areas she was trying to improve—especially in getting rid of "the look." One manager asked the important, but often unspoken, question, "And how would you like us to give you that feedback?"

This meeting represented significant progress for both the marketing director and her group of managers. The director boldly demonstrated her commitment to getting the news—positive or negative—about herself and her organization. She made it clear that she needed and wanted the support of those who work for her. And when she answered the question about how she wanted to receive the additional feedback, she paved the way for her managers to give her the support she needed to be successful.

In fact, that is exactly what occurred. In that same meeting, the group as a whole talked about their decision-making methods and the ways their habits contributed to the impression of top-down decision making in a department where there was a push toward self-managing teams. The group agreed that some of their collective patterns were a problem and made commitments to use different methods in the future. This change fulfilled a basic objective behind our client's introduction of the pilot teams.

In this case, the marketing director stopped short of saying that she expected each of her managers to seek feedback on their own management and communication styles. She also did not reaffirm the need to raise and solve problems collectively in order to improve. Her actions, however, demonstrated her belief in this approach. Her willingness to publicly receive personal feedback and discuss it with her subordinates set the stage for rewarding messengers throughout the department.

12

REDUCE AMBIGUOUS BEHAVIOR

In Chapter Six, "Behaviors That Create Fear," we identified the ambiguous behavior of supervisors and managers as a major source of tension. We described several kinds of confusing conduct that create tension and open the door to mistrust:

- Secretive decision making

- Uninviting behaviors

- Lack of, or indirect, communication

- Lack of responsiveness to suggestions

- Inconsistency and mixed messages

- Unethical conduct

Ambiguous behavior provokes fear because it does not provide needed, reliable information. The facts, issues, or intentions are absent, unclear, or contradictory. This lack of information triggers a chain of events that eventually leads to fear.

1. The employee sees the boss behaving in an ambiguous way.

2. The employee tries to interpret this unclear or insufficient information. This raises questions for the employee, such as the boss's intentions or the extent to which the employee is valued, trusted, or viewed as competent by the boss.

3. In the absence of additional information, the cycle of mistrust provides negative explanations for the ambiguous behavior.

4. The employee becomes anxious about what the ambiguous behaviors *might* mean, what is *really* expected by the boss, or what *could* happen.

In cases such as this, people frequently do not know what to do. They grope in darkness and worry about what will befall them. All they know is that they do not know; this leads to speculation, concern, and worst-case thinking. Unfortunately, when reliable information is unavailable people rely on the cycle of mistrust. The cycle is a ready reservoir of explanations for a mixed message, lack of feedback, or indirect communication. It encourages people to decipher in a negative way the unclarified who, what, why, and how. Lack of information, combined with negative assumptions and mistrust, causes people to be afraid.

Ambiguity is in the eye of the beholder. What one person sees as a practical, situational response, another views as suspicious inconsistency. One person might be confused about the accuracy of information, while another does not understand why the information was presented in the first place. While "no news is good news" for one work unit, for another it means that information is being hidden. Given the complexity of this response, is it possible for managers to overcome this problem of perceptions? Ironically, our answer is a mixed message. Yes, a lot can be done to create a clear flow of information throughout an organization. No, there will probably never be a time when things are not misinterpreted to some degree. Hence, the title of this chapter asks readers to *reduce* ambiguous behavior, rather than *eliminate* it.

The suggestions we offer to reduce ambiguous behavior are information oriented. They respond to the need of employees to know in clear terms what is meant by a particular communication, what is happening or likely to happen. They are organized around five simple principles of communication and involvement:

1. Invite people in and help them to feel welcome.

2. Give as much clear information as possible.

3. Listen to and respond to suggestions for action.

4. Involve people in decisions.

5. Do not put people into double-binds.

The straightforward nature of these principles belies the complexity of putting them into practice. In the sections that follow, we provide a variety of action steps which address the first, second, and last of these principles. Principle 3 is covered in Chapter Eleven, "Value Criticism: Reward the Messenger"; principle 4 in Chapter Fourteen, "Collaborate on Decisions." Our suggestions are *examples* of the ways the principles can be employed in everyday management practice, but they by no means cover all the possibilities. This collection of potential actions is intended to hit high points and stimulate thinking, not to cover every base.

INVITE PEOPLE IN AND HELP THEM TO FEEL WELCOME

Inviting people in is welcoming them. With words and actions they are made to feel important and equal. Just as when you welcome a new neighbor or invite someone to your home for the first time, there is a more personal sharing of information. It is communication that says, "I want to get to know you and I want you to get to know me." This getting-acquainted process is an essential base for ongoing relationships.

Let People Know How You Feel

In the current business environment, this is not necessarily an easy thing to do. Organizational environments are usually geared more to the head than the heart. People become oriented to using their time efficiently, taking action, and using their brains to solve problems. Talking about feelings is often regarded as a nonessential activity. In climbing the traditional corporate success ladder, some people may have learned to play their cards close to their chest. They have learned that to open up can be interpreted as a sign of naiveté or vulnerability—something that can damage their credibility and influence. And of course, as a matter of culture and temperament, some people are simply less outgoing than others. They are naturally less likely to disclose information about themselves or their feelings about issues at hand.

And yet employees want to know who their managers are. Their desire to get acquainted pertains to both work-related competencies and the personal values which guide decision making at work. They long for their bosses to behave like "real-life human beings" and are delighted when it happens. When you as a manager do not come across in a full, open sense, others do not know what to expect. If you and your values remain hidden, your employees will be left to speculate and interpret both your intentions and your behavior. They will then give you what they believe you want, which may not be what you are interested in at all.

Get close enough to people so that they get a keener, more immediate grasp of who you are as a person. This does not mean being friends with everyone, continually going out to lunch, or meeting each others' families. It does mean talking now and then about your feelings, values, and perceptions and encouraging others to talk about theirs. This can sometimes seem slow and unimportant but, in fact, it is a wise investment in personal credibility. In particular, use "feeling" terms, such as *elated, frustrated, disappointed, grateful, angry,* and *relieved.* These are words that tell in no uncertain terms where "you are coming from." Do not just talk about the program or the budget or the reorganization. Talk about how you *feel* about it, as well. Let people get to know you.

Make Time

Absence, in the business world, generally does not make the heart grow fonder. Just the opposite—it can cause people to feel unwelcome. A professional-level employee spoke with us about her boss, with whom she consulted for only one hour per month. She felt that it negatively influenced her performance to have so little contact. She wanted to be clearer about performance expectations and her role. She noticed that a co-worker seemed to have almost daily contact with their supervisor and that their discussions seemed more social. Her interpretation was that favoritism was at work and that she was disadvantaged because of it.

Situations like this one bring to mind one of the difficulties supervisors must manage: What is the balance between too much and too little intrusion into the work of subordinates? As the story here illustrates, this can be a problem of both amount and equity. There are individual differences in how much time a person would like with the boss and how much he or she is concerned about the closeness or distance of others.

First, solve the problem of the amount of time you spend with individuals. Ask people whether they are getting enough or too much of you. Develop a sense of their needs as individuals, and look for patterns in their responses. Get a sense of who will want more contact and who may prefer less. Do your best to accommodate these individual needs. Additionally, resolve the overall question of equity by creating a routine. For example, you might decide to meet with each individual once a month for two hours and have a Monday morning staff meeting where everyone is present. Follow through on this schedule. If an issue like favoritism is "hot" in your group, bring it out into the open and discuss it collectively. See the next chapter, "Discuss the Undiscussables," for advice on how to proceed.

Use a Process Check

One technique which is common to group process training and which helps people feel valued in group settings is called a "process check." This is just a stopping point, during or at the close of a meeting, which gives people a chance to talk about what they like, dislike, or have questions about. If strong concerns are voiced, decisions can be made about how to improve interaction—in the remaining part of the meeting or at the next meeting or encounter. The process check gives people a chance to talk about what has been left hanging. If people are still confused, the confusion almost always surfaces. If a problem has developed in a relationship during the meeting, the parties can reacknowledge their commitment to work it out.

All you need to do is stop conversation a moment and ask each person in the group for his or her reactions and questions. Or, in a less pointed fashion, use the following lead-ins to get people to volunteer their observations about the meeting:

> ❝ *How is this going so far? Are we getting at the things that are most important to you?* ❞

> ❝ *How is the pace? Are we going too fast? Too slow?* ❞

> ❝ *What would make this a better use of your time?* ❞

> ❝ *Are there any undiscussables that we've avoided here?* ❞

> ❝ *If we were to play this conversation over again, what might we do to improve it?* ❞

The process check can be used in one-on-one situations as well as with groups. It can be applied in person or over the telephone. It essentially consists of slowing down the process to see if people's needs are being met and if course corrections need to be made.

Use Common Courtesy

Keep in mind the importance of basic good manners. Graciousness in interpersonal dealings invites others to feel comfortable and valued. Good manners are signs of respect that are often neglected in the pace of a busy day.

- Say "please" and "thank you," and say "hello" when you see people in the hallway. If possible, call people by name.

- Do your fair share of loading paper in the copy machine or making or pouring coffee. Do not act like you are better than the others.

- Make genuine inquiries about people's weekends and vacations.

- Acknowledge success or discouragement with honest enthusiasm or empathy.

These are examples of little things that are remembered as indicators of real personality and motives. They imply sensitivity, concern, and respect for others. They tell people that you do not take yourself too seriously and that you do value the roles others play. To be effective, of course, these small but powerful interactions must be sincere.

Give as Much Clear Information as Possible

There are two questions related to information flow that managers would be wise to consider:

- What information should I share and with whom?

- What methods are best to ensure a fast and consistent flow of information throughout the organization?

These two concerns have a direct link to the amount of fear or trust that is present in the work environment. Access to accurate and timely information is a primary factor in making people feel included, valued, and trusted. Lack of access, or information that is wrong or late, creates the opposite effect.

Make Sure the Mail Gets Through

Having worked with employee communication issues for years, we are always surprised at the various time frames by which information is communicated downward. In one department a memo from the executive arrives on the front lines within an hour of its distribution to department heads. In other cases, it does not make it at all. Those who inherit their news from the grapevine rather than their boss usually wonder what this pattern means. Being left out of the official information loop sets people up to feel excluded, as symbolized by the popular definition of "mushroom management": a philosophy of "keeping people in the dark and heaping manure on them."

The problem may be one of efficiencies rather than negative intentions. The supervisor's office may be so clogged with technical tasks and requirements that it takes a week's turnaround to get mail down to the next layer of the organization. That is not how the situation will be read, however. People are most likely to perceive this as a more intentional put-down of those on the front lines who "do not need to know." That negative assumption, which properly belongs to the cycle of mistrust, may be mirrored by the past behavior of managers who honestly felt that people on the front lines should have very limited access to information. To improve your communication:

1. Assume the positive about your employees; believe that they are interested in what is going on and will put any information you

give them to good use. Decide if there is any good reason to with-
hold information. If there is none, share it with as many people
as possible who will be affected by it. If your "good reason" is
grounded in negative assumptions about employees, consider breaking the cycle of mistrust by passing along the information you might
otherwise have withheld.

2. Use electronic-mail and voice-mail systems to get information to
people quickly and in a consistent manner. Follow up on such messages in person, since without dialogue the communication will
remain one-way and thus limited.

3. Ask people what type of information they need to do quality work
and to feel good about the organization. Find out the kind of information which causes stress for individuals and work groups if it
is not provided. For ongoing issues, ask how often the information
is needed. Once this assessment is complete, do your best to provide
people with what they want and need.

For example, in one research project funded through yearly grants
of federal money, funding updates were included on the agenda of
every staff meeting, even though there was frequently no news to
report. Given the volatile nature of their funding source, staff members
appreciated knowing that there was no change. The project director
also agreed that as a standard practice, whenever she received any type
of news regarding future funding, she would pass it along to staff members in the form of a handwritten note that was duplicated and distributed on the spot.

Managers caught in the cycle of mistrust want loyalty and commitment without information. They literally ask for "blind" obedience.
Instead we see people giving their best work and long-term loyalty
to organizations that trust employees. Bringing people quickly into the
information loop about critical issues is a symbolic and practical way
to do this. Such sharing of information contributes to a sense of community and teamwork.

Decode Confusing Systems

Many management and personnel systems appear to be black boxes
to people. There is no way to see inside them to get a picture of how
things really work. Pay systems, performance appraisals, job placement,
terminations, and budgeting are just a few of the systems that can be
problematic because of their complexity and the actual or presumed

need for confidentiality. Ambiguous behavior, in conjunction with mysterious systems, can create a fearful combination. This does not just apply to personnel systems but to other business issues and legal matters as well. When you cannot explain what is happening, people will still be watching your behavior. If it is impossible to comment, at least acknowledge that you cannot communicate about a specific problem.

A supervisor we know was faced with a difficult job reclassification issue. Her employee, a skilled administrative assistant in a highly visible office, had asked that her job be upgraded. When the position was evaluated by staff in the human resources department, the employee's job was discovered to be three levels too low. While a promotion was clearly in order, advancing her to the level of her current work would have caused internal political problems. In working with the human resources department, the supervisor decided that the job should be reclassified to a level one step lower than the one the assistant had expected. The supervisor announced the new classification at a staff meeting, without consulting with the employee first. Due to the many projects assigned to her and other unfortunate time constraints, the supervisor was unable to talk to the employee about the decision in detail for several weeks. The assistant did not understand why the job was reclassified the way it had been and simply had to wait for the explanation.

We can only imagine how this looked and felt to the employee. She reported that she got much less work done during this time period, experienced considerable self-doubts, and had many questions about the meaning of her boss's behavior. She wanted very much to talk with her boss to find out why the reclassification was lower than she believed it ought to be. However, she was afraid that the supervisor might think she was challenging her, and so out of fear for her reputation she did not confront her. She also did not want to impair any future reclassification efforts. Instead, she talked to others in her office and consulted with human resources staff. While nothing malicious or negative was intended on the supervisor's part, the ambiguity of her conduct and her lack of information about the decision created tension and a loss of credibility. It surely triggered fear, anger, and frustration for the administrative assistant. To avoid situations like this, consider the following actions:

1. In situations where you are not inhibited by legal or procedural restraints, act quickly to let people know what is happening. Be sensitive to their worries about what your silence means and to the ways in which it can be misconstrued. With the administrative assis-

tant's reclassification, the supervisor made a significant error in not immediately talking to her about the politics involved in her situation. In a better world, she would have talked with the employee first, before announcing the reclassification to the rest of the staff. She would have helped the assistant to understand the office dynamics, talked about her feelings, and discussed whether or not future efforts at reclassification were feasible. The supervisor certainly would not have delayed the discussion until several weeks after the announcement.

2. At other times, when it is impossible to communicate openly about a specific issue, say so to the people most affected by the situation. Ask that they understand the sensitive circumstances and support you as you work with the issue in an appropriate and confidential manner. Let people know *why* you are withholding information. Is it to protect someone's privacy or the company's competitive advantage? Are you doing it on the advice of corporate attorneys? Knowing that the matter is intentionally closed and that there is a good reason for doing this avoids the assumption that you do not trust or want to include your subordinates in your work.

3. Acknowledge and respond to the perceptions that can grow up quickly in such an environment. When rumors come to your attention, correct misinformation immediately. Remember that rumors are a common part of organizational life, and ask to be informed about them as they surface. Consider them as opportunities to explore undiscussable issues.

Answer People's Questions

Especially in times of change, people need to have their questions answered. The trick, of course, if they are not voicing their concerns is knowing which issues to address. Thus, two skills become very helpful: anticipating questions someone might have and sensing when questions remain unanswered even after discussion. There are several techniques that can help you in this process:

1. In your communication, cover the basic *who, what, why,* and *when* questions. Talk about the long-term and short-term benefits of the change, as well as the problems you anticipate. Give background information and take extra time to allow people to understand the circumstances or reasoning behind a particular approach or decision. Think about yourself when you are in the subordinate role.

What questions do you typically want answered by your bosses? Make sure there is time set aside for discussion so that communication is two-way.

2. Slow down in order to practice a slightly more deliberate form of communication with those who report to you. Recognize that frequently *effective* communication and *efficient* communication are not represented by the same conversation. While content—the *what, why,* and *who*—is essential, many people need a more leisurely discussion of the implications, feelings, and future directions associated with any particular issue. This is particularly true if emotions are high and fear is present. Be prepared to shift from content to process issues, based upon what you hear from others.

3. In the midst of such discussions, ask good process questions as a means of finding out what else needs to be talked about. Sometimes these are similar to the process check described earlier in this chapter, but other, broader questions about how work is going can be included. Some examples are

" *Now, where are we?* "

" *Can you give me your understanding of my position on this issue?* "

" *What is it we have agreed upon?* "

" *What still needs to be resolved?* "

" *What will happen as a result of this meeting? When? Who will do it?* "

" *When do we check in again on this project?* "

" *How shall we communicate what we have agreed upon to others?* "

" *What else do we need to talk about?* "

" *Have we left anything out?* "

These and many other similar process questions will help take the drift out of your dealings with others and lead to clean, clear outcomes. They are all based on the principles of open feedback and convey the thought, "We are all in this together."

Let People Know Where They Stand

Because people want to do quality work, they want to know where they stand with their bosses. They want to know how they are doing in terms of the quality of their work, their productivity, and their relationships with others in their work environment. And they want ideas on how to improve in all these areas. When people do not know what is expected and do not get feedback regularly about how they are doing, they have a hard time improving their performance and they often become anxious. Without performance feedback, by definition, people are working in an ambiguous work environment.

These points have been made so often by others, and are such a common component of basic management texts, that we hesitate to give them more attention here. Consider the following statements as reminders of things effective managers do. More information about how to give ongoing performance feedback and conduct formal appraisals is typically available from a human resources department and through libraries, bookstores, or short training sessions.

- Remember that performance feedback is more than an appraisal. It needs to be an ongoing part of the supervisor-employee relationship and should be present on a daily basis. The key phrase is "no surprises within formal appraisals."

- Be clear about what you want from your employees. If you cannot articulate what your desires and expectations are, employees will have to second guess your wishes.

- Sharpen your skills at describing behavior in neutral terms.

- Make feedback a two-way street; allow others to share their perceptions of your performance with you.

- Conduct formal appraisals on time. Late appraisals are a classic example of ambiguous behavior.

Do Not Put People into Double-Binds

Double-binds not only create tension; they also immobilize people, making them less capable of exhibiting the initiative and judgment that organizations need. A double-bind asks people to do something that compromises their values and sets them up for confusion, disappointment, or failure. They demand that a person act in a certain way while simultaneously creating barriers to behaving in that way. There are two major kinds of double-bind: sending mixed messages and asking others to operate unethically.

Recognize and Acknowledge the Mixed Messages You Send

Given the complexity of organizational life, even the best-skilled and best-intentioned managers are likely to put out mixed messages from time to time. Classics include:

66 *Yes, use discretion, but no, don't make any mistakes.* 99

66 *By all means, consider new approaches, but be careful not to contradict established policies.* 99

66 *Do what's necessary—just make sure you stay in budget.* 99

Mixed messages feel like riddles handed off to others with the command, "You figure it out." They cause anyone who hears them to instinctively say, "Wait a minute. What do you *really* mean?" While they are far easier to recognize from the listener's perspective, it is also important for managers, as senders, to recognize and acknowledge their own mixed messages. This enables managers to cut down on the number of confusing, ambiguous messages they send and minimize the impact of those they do. To avoid mixed messages:

1. Pay attention to what you are really asking your employees to do. Are you sending contradictory messages in your requests or expectations? Do you impose limitations or restrictions that will make it impossible for an employee to do what you ask? Listen for the conditions you impose when you make an assignment. They may be the clue that you are asking someone to do two incompatible things at once.

2. When you hear yourself making ambiguous statements or recognize that your nonverbal behavior may be saying one thing while your words give another message, acknowledge what is going on. Admit that you are saying two things simultaneously or are confused, caught between two conflicting values. Ask for patience and cooperation in "walking both sides of the street at the same time." Engage your employees in strategy discussions about the political, opera-

tional, and human realities that have created this situation and ask how you can manage the dilemma together.

Ask People to Highlight Mixed Messages

No matter how hard you try, it is not likely that you will be able to catch all the mixed messages you send. If others can help you recognize this situation when it occurs, you will be able to address the confusion together. This means that people will need to give you feedback when they feel caught on the horns of the dilemma. Use the following techniques:

1. Talk with your work group about the pattern of mixed messages in the organization. Explain the pressures and political realities that sometimes cause you to ask people to do two opposing things at once. Talk about their perspectives on the issue. Is it a big problem? What kind of confusion, frustration, anxiety, or fear does it cause for them? What patterns do they see in your behavior?

2. Say that you would like help in identifying mixed messages and you need their assistance. If you sense that your employees might be reluctant to give such direct feedback to you, suggest the following formula. When people hear you give a mixed message, they can say, "I hear you saying _____ but I see you doing _____," or "I hear you asking me to _____ but at the same time you want me to _____."

   When a group adopts a specific method like this to say difficult things, it creates a special code for conveying feedback. Agreements like this can make it easier for others to get used to giving you feedback. They also give others a sanctioned approach that they can use with each other and that you can use with them. Be aware that this exercise can open some threatening doors for people. If your situation is extreme and you know that there is a large amount of fear and mistrust in the work group, do not hesitate to bring in an outside facilitator to assist you.

Using either of these two techniques, you may receive feedback on a host of issues—anything from your personal style to new computers. Once you have clarified and understood the feedback, engage the group in a problem-solving discussion in which all members contribute suggestions and action plans. Keeping the exercise as descriptive and non-judgmental as possible will help you to control any defensiveness you might be inclined to express.

Asking others to highlight the mixed messages they hear can yield enormous clues about what people see as inconsistencies. For example, you may learn that people see a major discrepancy between abrasive behavior of managers to employees and a demand for warm, friendly customer relations. Or they may think that current belt-tightening measures and staff reductions are related to the recent refurbishing of executives' offices.

The dilemmas which are highlighted can provide exceptional feedback to managers about the measures and explanations needed to build support from employees. In other cases, the dilemmas may not be entirely resolvable. But as the systems and business issues behind them are explored, people may come to understand and appreciate the complicated circumstances you and the organization face. And, in the long run, this effort may lead to some truly innovative solutions.

Do Not Ask People to Act Unethically

Our interviews and experience tell us that only rarely do managers ask employees to do something ethically wrong. What is more likely is that a request creates a conflict in values for the employee and is thus perceived to be unethical. In such situations, the individual is caught between the boss's demands, the organization's code of conduct, and the person's own sense of integrity.

For example, in one public agency employees told us that they were told to advise citizens that a certain service was not available, but they were not to indicate that this was the result of lack of money. In fact, no other explanation seemed reasonable, so employees did not know what else to say. This was heard by employees as asking them to lie to the agency's customers about its services. This situation created ambiguity and a tremendous frustration for employees. They could not carry out the management's request without feeling compromised in some way. There are two ways to counteract this type of situation:

1. Anticipate when requests you make of your employees might push them into an ethical dilemma. Although people certainly vary in terms of their adherence to basic values, common situations to avoid include asking employees to knowingly do things which cause them to

   - Lie or hide the truth
   - Manipulate resources or people
   - Take or use things that do not belong to them

- Hurt others
- Break or bend the law or established policies
- Say one thing and do another

2. As with mixed messages, if you find that you must ask employees to do things which might put them in a compromising situation, let them know that you are aware of the dilemma you are creating. Explore the situation with them so they understand the competing circumstances you face. If possible, allow them to choose their level of participation. For example, in a hospital, an employee had to wheel abortion patients to the operating room. This violated his personal values. The supervisor was able to arrange for him to work with other cases.

If there is no choice—if you must have their involvement—let them know how much you appreciate their support. If they choose to leave your work group or the organization rather than go along with what you need them to do, help them to make this transition with their integrity intact. Situations such as this can become extraordinarily complex to manage. Keeping communication as honest and open as possible will help to reduce the confusion and minimize fear.

Given the complexity of any workday, there are continuous opportunities for managers to behave in ambiguous and confusing ways. Because of its slippery nature, this aspect of managerial performance is difficult to evaluate and hard to target. The suggestions we have provided are offered as a place to begin. The goal is to reduce the number of inaccurate, confusing, or incomplete communications which cause people to get caught in the cycle of mistrust.

13

DISCUSS
THE
UNDISCUSSABLES

One of the best and most powerful ways to begin overcoming fear's influence is to discuss the undiscussables. It is a rich technique for accessing the hidden issues and problems covered up in relationships, work groups, and the organization as a whole. As with all the strategies we present, discussing the undiscussables is not a one-time event. It certainly can be an excellent approach for a retreat or special problem-solving meeting, as we will explain. But it is also a principle of disclosure that should become a part of everyday communication.

This chapter offers a variety of ideas that you can use to reduce the number of undiscussables in your work environment. It specifically presents three concrete approaches for using the concept of undiscussables in team development. Additionally, the chapter addresses some of the "hard-core" undiscussables that may be at the root of fear-oriented work environments. While we focus on undiscussables in group contexts, we hope that the information provided will also encourage you and members of your team to talk about undiscussables in one-on-one relationships. Even though we most frequently refer to group situations, the techniques we suggest are also applicable to individual settings unless we specify otherwise.

As you put our suggestions to work, remember that undiscussables should be treated with respect. Uncovering what people are not talking about and why they are not talking requires sensitivity. Such discussions frequently involve self-esteem, private work anxieties, and strong feelings such as anger or frustration. People take their undiscussables personally. Yet given the right environment and the right manager, individuals can become remarkably open about issues which may have been hidden for a long time.

We generally suggest that groups or individuals adopt the following sequence when they begin to address undiscussables:

- Introduce the concept.
- Identify the undiscussables.
- Talk about them.
- Take appropriate follow-up action.

The first thing to do is to decide how you would like to introduce others to the concept of undiscussable issues. There are many options. We present three that show different levels of involvement. The approach you choose needs to match the current trust levels among members of your team. Your approach should push a little on people's comfort zones without overwhelming them.

THE INFORMAL INTRODUCTION

One low-key method is to simply raise the idea of discussing undiscussables and see what happens. You will be modeling what it is like to bring up a sensitive topic.

One way to do this is by talking about one of your own undiscussables. In the course of operational problem solving with your team, you might informally use the concept to get at a hidden point. A discussion might take the following form:

"Let's go back and talk about scheduling for a minute," you say. "I get the feeling that some of these project costs have become undiscussable for us."

"What do you mean, 'undiscussable'?" questions one of the group.

"I mean that they are something people are feeling hesitant to talk about in this room with those who can help to resolve the issue," you reply, pausing.

"Well," says somebody else, "those costs might be *a little* outrageous."

To begin this approach you will need to identify an issue which you or others might be worried about discussing. If it is one where someone might possibly perceive some type of repercussion, you've found yourself a likely undiscussable. By raising such an issue in this way, you reassure your team that it is acceptable to talk about sensitive issues. You communicate that openness is valued. And you and your team develop a track record for dealing successfully with a sticky point.

James Kouzes and Barry Posner would call this approach one of creating a succession of "small wins" (1988, pp. 217–218). They point out that "getting commitment to new behaviors, like solving big problems, is often overwhelming." They suggest, as an alternative, more incremental change processes to "break down big problems into doable steps" which reward people with positive feelings as they reach obvious milestones.

Using the concept this way gets the ball rolling. If you sprinkle the idea into your day-to-day dealings, people will soon begin applying the term "undiscussable" on their own. Notice that you have not introduced the concept of fear—*why* things are undiscussable—at all. This quick and easy approach works because people instinctively know what undiscussables are. They also instinctively dislike them and welcome opportunities to get them out in the open.

DIRECTLY INTRODUCE THE CONCEPT

The next level of involvement requires you to use the concept of undiscussables in a more direct fashion.

Brief Your Group on Undiscussable Issues

Explain to the group that you want to create a more open environment where people talk freely about work-related problems. Tell them you are intrigued by some new ideas to help teams develop and are interested in getting their reactions. Use Tables 2 and 3 on pages 31 and 43 to summarize our findings about typical undiscussables and why people don't speak up. Then ask the group two questions:

> 66 *In what ways do these findings mirror or differ from your own experience of organizations in general?* 99

> 66 *To what degree do these findings reflect our own organization/division/work group?* 99

Their responses may give you some strong clues about their readiness to proceed to more open levels of discussion. In answering the second question, you may only get some vague suggestions for improvement, such as, "We need to get together before problems get too big." But you may also observe some nodding heads and silent understanding. Some members of the team may be saying to themselves, "Boy, if you only knew!"

Our experience at this level of discussion is that sometimes people will lean toward denial. They will say things like "I really don't think we have this kind of problem," "This is a great place to work," or "You are a great boss." If this happens:

1. Accept these comments and say supportively, "Thank you. I'm glad you feel so positively. I want to make sure that feeling always stays with us. I wonder, though, what we—or I—can do to improve things."

2. Don't push hard. Let the conversation develop naturally. Be patient and don't overtalk. Tell the team you are inviting them to use the concept in their interactions with you and with each other.

3. One additional step at this level is to ask them to keep a list of some of the undiscussable issues they discover in the next few weeks. Explain the rest of this exercise as described here:

   - Team members' lists should be based on the types of undiscussables shown in Table 2 on page 31.

   - Generalities are all that is necessary.

   - The undiscussables they discover can be ones they feel personally or ones they have heard about from others which pertain to the broader organization.

Arrange the agenda of your next meeting so there is plenty of time to fully discuss this topic. We recommend one to two hours.

At the follow-up meeting, have people report on the kind of issues they have seen as undiscussable. This is most easily done through a voting process with a list of the potential undiscussables on a flipchart. Once people have voted, refocus on why the issues were undiscussable. Was there fear of repercussions? A sense that speaking up would be useless? Get people to talk about their feelings concerning the undiscussables. Ask what the team could and should be doing differently to keep undiscussables from arising. Invite people to communicate with you directly on any issues relating to your leadership style.

FOCUS ON THE UNDISCUSSABLES OF YOUR GROUP

The third approach goes much farther than either of the two previous formats. It is an open-ended exploration of the full range of undiscussables in a work team. Because of the way it is structured, a qualified process consultant or group facilitator is necessary to help carry it out. It is to be used *only* with groups experienced with team-building events, where all members voluntarily and collaboratively decide to pursue this avenue to team development. Everyone should be present at the event; it lasts one to two days and can be an excellent kickoff to a broad transformation of the organization. Here is how it works.

Before the retreat, the process consultant privately interviews each member of the team of people who immediately report to you. The consultant consolidates the data from everyone interviewed into key themes and arranges them as a matrix, shown in Figure 6.

This matrix then becomes a tool for analysis by the team. The leader and members collaboratively select priority areas for improvement, discuss the nature of the problems, and decide what needs to happen. Usually, the work continues through several meetings, with periodic follow-up sessions.

This is a powerful technique. In one company, a team of middle managers and their leader identified the following issues for further work based on their matrix:

- Questions about the leader's tenure as head of the organization
- Failure of the leader to share his goals with the team

- Questions about the degree of autonomy to be granted to branch offices

- Perceived favoritism in the way particular divisions had been granted resources

- Conflict and suspicion between two members of the management team

This was more than enough to deal with. Although the first three issues could be settled quickly, the last two were much tougher and required longer-term action plans. In particular, the issue of favoritism ultimately resulted in an extensive employee survey and group meetings between the managers and employees.

A narrower version of this event could be constructed where the focus is on a particular business or operational problem. For example, the team might decide to evaluate project management systems, the budgeting process, the quality improvement effort, or other major initiatives. Team members volunteer information in three categories: strengths of the program, current needs and opportunities for improvement, and undiscussables. The assistance of an outside facilitator is also helpful with this more focused application.

HANDLE UNDISCUSSABLES WITH CARE

To get the best from discussing undiscussables:

1. Create a safe, blame-free environment. People will talk easily about undiscussables when they are asked in a sincere, natural way. Ensure confidentiality and sufficient time for a response.

2. Accept the undiscussables, whatever they are. Take a nonjudgmental approach. Explore what each issue means to people and how they feel about it. Clarify the issues; share relevant facts, feelings, or perceptions; and identify any necessary changes in behavior, systems, or practices.

3. Remember that not every undiscussable raised by a group needs to be dealt with in a group setting. How a member's family situation or drinking problem affects the work can be better handled through one-on-one coaching plus referral to an employee assistance program or an appropriate agency. If such an issue comes up, tell the group that they have raised a legitimate issue, but one that cannot

	What is undiscussable?	Why is it undiscussed?	What impact does that have?
With the manager (you)			
With peers in the work team			
With those who report to members of the team			
Within the organization as a whole			

Figure 6.   Undiscussables Matrix

be resolved by them. Encourage respect for the employee's privacy and feelings. Reassure the others that appropriate action will be taken to help the employee, and make sure it does. If the employee is present when the issue arises in the group, follow up later to discuss with the person his or her feelings about the meeting.

4. Remember that if a personal circumstance surfaces that has no impact on work, it is simply not a germane matter. As part of its definition, an undiscussable is an issue that—because it is not discussed—has a negative impact on quality, productivity, or job satisfaction.

5. When using a special problem-solving meeting or retreat to discuss undiscussables, be sure to set ground rules. The goal is to discuss work-related issues in a constructive, mutually supportive way. Discussing the undiscussables is not like being in an encounter group. Remind people that the purpose of discussion is to identify work-oriented problems in order to move forward together, not to place blame.

6. Do not use the concept of undiscussables to deal with an issue you ought to be managing personally. If you know that one of your subordinates is having significant performance problems, coach and supervise. Do not set up a "discuss the undiscussables" event which unnecessarily highlights that person's performance failings or uses peer feedback as blackmail.

HANDLING THE "NOW WHATS?"

Once an undiscussable issue has been brought to the surface, the group—or you and the individual you are working with—then needs to investigate the topic and develop ideas about how the undiscussable will be addressed. Many groups spontaneously begin to generate ideas and suggestions, but others may need a little help. You might want to use a technique originated by Weyerhaeuser executive Fred Fosmire called *STP,* standing for *Situation, Target, Proposal.* It is a simple brainstorming technique that fosters collaborative problem solving (see Figure 7).

Have people freely brainstorm their thoughts about the undiscussable while one member of the group records their ideas on a flipchart or blackboard.

- *Target* ideas represent possible outcomes, ideals, values, hopes, and wishes.

- *Situation* observations tell about what is happening now, the current status of things, and opinions about what is causing the present dilemma.

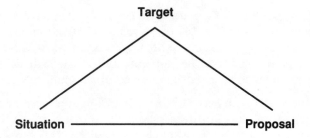

Figure 7. STP Brainstorming

- *Proposals* are means to get from the situation to the target. They are methods, action steps, or techniques for achieving the goal.

The clear advantage of this technique is that after a few minutes some patterns may become obvious. Perhaps there is more focus on the current situation without having a target in mind. Perhaps the target is clear but no one has made any proposals. The group begins to monitor its own problem-solving trends and naturally moves toward action steps that have a defined goal—all based upon issues once thought undiscussable.

ACTION PLANS AND FOLLOW-UP

Many undiscussables require some type of follow-up action. There are usually two varieties: changes in interpersonal behavior and changes in work systems. In either case it is a good idea for those involved to agree on the steps that need to take place and a time and location for the follow-up. For example:

- If Bob needs to be more communicative with other department heads, how does he do this? What will he do in the next week, the next month?

- If the performance appraisal system is decried as the source of countless pay inequities, who will be responsible for fixing it? What method of correction will be employed? Who will be involved? When will you talk about this next?

- If perceptions of top-down decision making have haunted the department for the last three years, what actions will you and your team take to reverse that perception? How will more participative methods be implemented? How will decisions be explained so that there is less confusion and mistrust?

As the leader, you play a key role in making sure these action plans are followed up. It is not necessary for you to do all the work, but your visible support will most likely be required. This support means contact and follow-up action; for example, it may include

- Talking to Bob about his new efforts at communicating with his peers

- Making sure the discussions about performance appraisal include all the key organizational players

- Creating time out of busy meeting schedules to talk about the habits that reinforce an impression of top-down decision making

The collaboration needs to continue past the planning stage. Periodic meetings are vital to discuss progress and talk about how barriers can be overcome.

Getting together to review plans and progress is essential for the team as a whole. This is also true when you are working one on one. Follow-up meetings remind people of what they have learned and what they have made commitments to do. They are a chance to celebrate success and renew energy. As a checkpoint they often result in practical modifications or refinements of action plans. Your role is critical in making sure these follow-ups happen. Model commitment by following through on the changes and steps you have personally agreed to. If you do not do those things, what message are you sending?

WORKING WITH HARD-CORE UNDISCUSSABLES

Dealing with undiscussables is like peeling an onion or examining the cross-section of a tree trunk. Work groups will find layers of issues. The ones farthest from the surface are typically the hardest—and sometimes the most important—to discuss.

A few layers down, you are likely to find a predictable set of undiscussables. These can include the presence of fear; actual, perceived, or imagined repercussions; a sense of powerlessness; your management style; personnel systems; organizational norms; and perceptions of top management. This familiar list, first presented in Chapter Six, sticks like glue, lingering in the organization and reinforcing a general climate of fear. As such, it represents the hard-core undiscussables. If you can openly deal with these items, you'll probably be able to talk about most other concerns.

Often a sense of powerlessness is one of the first things to surface. As team members look down the list of things that are not discussed, they will feel that some of these items—perhaps some of the most important—cannot be changed. This should be viewed as another opportunity for team development.

Focus the Group

Have the group answer two key questions:

- Which of the undiscussables can we influence or control?
- Which of the undiscussables are outside our range of influence or control?

Answering these questions helps a group channel its energy to barriers that can be overcome, rather than issues over which it has no control. For example:

- Changing the manpower allocation may be next to impossible, but working on time schedules for existing personnel may be an immediate option.

- Bringing on part-time staff to cover an unanticipated workload may be in someone else's budget authority, but a work group could present an analysis of the issues to that person with recommendations for action.

- Changing a boss's management style may represent a big undertaking, but a group could provide specific targeted feedback requesting uninterrupted staff meetings and seek agreement on this one issue.

By taking action on the undiscussables, a group has the capacity to overcome cynicism. This is especially true when the effort results in concrete plans the team itself can carry out. The process of looking at issues concerning power and influence usually convinces people they have more of them than they had first imagined. Rachman's work, mentioned in Chapter Two, reflects this sense as he defines *helplessness* as the experience which results "from an acquired sense of futility" (1978, p. 7). As people come to grips with the fact that they *can* have an influence and commit to a plan of action, cynicism, powerlessness, and dependency have less room to grow.

Use Powerlessness as a Bridge to Explore Other Areas

When the issue of powerlessness surfaces, the stage is often set to examine some of the other hard-core issues. The following questions may prompt high-risk yet highly important discussions:

" *Which of the barriers to our influence or control relate to systems in the organization? To personnel systems in particular? Which relate to the general way we go about doing things around here?* "

" *When people talk about powerlessness, how much of that reflects a cynicism about management in general? About top management? About me?* "

" *How many of the undiscussable items reflect a fear of repercussions? What kind of repercussions? What is our evidence for believing this is the case? What influence do we have to get rid of these repercussions?* "

Such questions can lead the group to a new level of communication and may result in another layer of undiscussable events as yet undisclosed. As people search for the sources of their feelings, they may uncover past events: an experience at the negotiating table, a derogatory comment from an upper-level manager, a negative experience with a co-worker, or something else which still operates behind their feelings. Individuals have a chance to test their own perceptions against the general assessment of the group and determine for themselves whether their private anxieties are justified. As with all undiscussables, bringing the hard-core issues into the bright light of group discussion reduces their mysterious power and usually proves them to be normal-sized concerns quite capable of being resolved.

By being willing to discuss the hard-core issues, and particularly repercussions, you and your team will be addressing the most common fears of people at work. As manager, you will be demonstrating in a very genuine way that you do not discount people's fears. You are removing the labels, judgments, and loss of credibility that traditionally go with speaking up about repercussions.

Acknowledging that the fear of repercussions may be based in reality affirms perception and judgment. It means that you, as leader, are willing to consider information collaboratively and hunt with others for the facts of particular situations. On the surface, this may not seem like anything radical. But in organizations where people have avoided undiscussables for years, such action can represent a significant new trend.

Talking about the hard-core undiscussables is a vital point in the effort to reduce fear, because it deals with the reasons why people do not speak up. It addresses these fears directly, bringing a new openness to communication within your immediate work environment.

THE ONGOING SEARCH

Carrying out the foregoing steps is likely to institutionalize the concept of undiscussables. The concept will surface from time to time in conversation as an introduction to a sensitive topic, a red flag on an issue that needs attention. This ongoing search for undiscussables becomes a means to ensure that trust is continually being built. It helps guarantee that new, better ways of doing things are not quashed under the weight of some possible repercussion or the conclusion that speaking up will do no good. You and your team will find yourselves talking about concerns as they come up, long before they become sensitive and frightening topics. In such cases you will no doubt observe the delightful irony that the more you are able to talk about undiscussables, the fewer there will be to discuss.

14

COLLABORATE

ON

DECISIONS

Decision-making
processes are at the core of organizational
life. Responsibility for particular decisions determines the nature of jobs and
roles; the power structure and hierarchy;
peer, boss, and subordinate relations;
one's influence on others; and, thus, the
organization. In this chapter we offer an
easy-to-use model for decision making

---

and a variety of suggestions on how to increase collaboration in your work group. More specifically, we suggest ideas about

- Becoming aware of current decision-making patterns
- Seeking input on decisions
- Group process issues
- Moving from participation to collaboration
- Managing consensus
- Communicating about decisions that have been made
- The role of the leader in this process

The patterns of decision making have enormous impact on how people think and feel. Concerns about this area appeared throughout our interviews in a variety of ways. For example, of the behaviors that generate fear, secretive decision making was singled out as a critical component of ambiguous behavior, one of fear's four key arenas. When people have been left out of decisions, they often feel powerless and unneeded. They become dependent on others, anxious about their value to the organization, cynical in their dealings, and understandably resistant to well-intentioned efforts to "empower" people. This leads them to experience the meaning of Peter Block's expression: "I fear those that I feel dependent on" (1987, p. 10).

There is increasing pressure on anyone in a leadership role today to involve people in decisions. Our work force is now composed of people who expect to participate. Management theory has evolved over the last forty years to encourage participative and delegated decisions. For many managers it is taken as an article of faith that

- Those who make the product or provide the service have essential information necessary for improving quality and making sound decisions.

- People who have some say in decisions that affect them are much more likely to carry out those decisions with enthusiasm and effectiveness.

And yet, from our interviews and what we see with our clients, we have come to believe that many managers are unconscious and somewhat unskilled in decision making, particularly when it requires collaboration between levels of an organization. They are frequently unclear about the real decision that needs to be made, how it is to be made, and who to involve. It is not uncommon for managers who see themselves as open and participative to be viewed by those who work for them as top-down managers who are inconsistent in the way they handle decisions. In such cases, unclear or misunderstood decision making causes mistrust, confusion, miscommunication, a sense of powerlessness, and alienation. As the many stories we have told in previous chapters attest, where feelings such as these exist, fear is not far behind.

A SIMPLE MODEL FOR DECISION MAKING

There are a variety of models that help individuals and groups to be more effective in their decision making. The one in Figure 8 has been used successfully with a variety of clients. It was developed several years ago as part of an effort to help the leadership group of a 600-member city department better understand employee complaints about decision making. The model modifies Tannenbaum and Schmidt's well-known "Leadership Styles Continuum" (1957, p. 96). We also use a continuum, but we have five points on our scale, rather than seven.

There are essentially five methods by which leaders make decisions. By the term *leader,* we mean the person responsible for making sure the decision is made.

- In method 1, the leader makes the decision alone.

- In method 2, the leader makes the decision with limited input. This input is informal and unplanned—the person the leader has lunch with, carpools with, or meets with late on a Thursday afternoon, or a next-door neighbor.

- In method 3, the leader makes the decision with consciously designed input. Here the leader assembles a plan that will gather

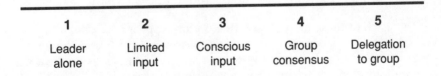

1	2	3	4	5
Leader alone	Limited input	Conscious input	Group consensus	Delegation to group

Source. Adapted from Tannenbaum and Schmidt, 1957.

Figure 8.   Five-Point Decision-Making Model

helpful input, considering who will be affected by the decision; various expertise, experience, and values that need to be heard; representation of different levels of the organization; who will be important in implementing this decision; and the data relating to the issue to be decided. We use the term *participative* to describe this type of decision making.

- In method 4, the leader and the group make the decision together. This is what we refer to as *collaborative* decision making. With this method, the leader may initiate the decision-making process but essentially operates as an equal member of the team. Usually people get together in one room to make the decision. Sometimes a facilitator is called in so the leader is able to fully participate as an equal member of the group. The group operates from a consensus model, in which members work together so that decisions are acceptable to all. This does not mean that everyone is in total agreement, but all members do agree that the decisions made will guide their individual actions. We recommend "what we can agree to so we can move forward together" as an operational definition of consensus.

- In method 5, the leader delegates the decision to a group. In this last method, the group collectively makes the decision without the leader being present. In such situations, the leader turns the issue that needs a decision over to the appropriate group and establishes the group's authority. If the leader has restrictions or minimum requirements for the way in which the decision is made or the expected outcomes, they should be identified and understood up front. After that, the group handles the decision in whatever way it sees fit—usually modeling method 4, consensus only, without the leader. The leader becomes reinvolved only if the decision appears to be significantly off-track or if it negatively influences issues outside the group's sphere of knowledge. Otherwise, the group is considered responsible for the decision.

Each of these methods is effective and appropriate depending on the situation. *There is no one right way.* We have found, however, that many organizations are interested in pushing decisions toward methods 4 and 5. In one client organization, this was described with the graph in Figure 9.

The point is that not all decisions are made according to methods 4 and 5, but more are being made in that way than have been in the past. This gradual transition toward more collaborative methods is one

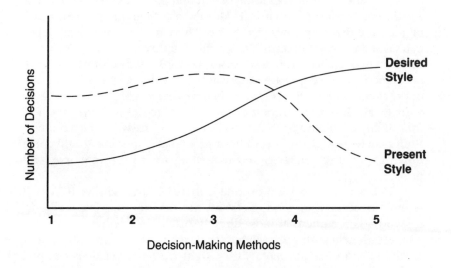

Figure 9.   Trends Toward Collaboration

that many managers can immediately understand and aim for. The traditional worry that participative methods mean a loss of power or control is mitigated by knowing that not every operational situation or urgent dilemma becomes a group decision. The focus is on finding opportunities to move method 2 decisions toward methods 3 and 4, and method 3 toward methods 4 and 5, when the leader determines that this is appropriate. Generally, this shift occurs slowly as people adjust to new methods and develop their skills.

WORRIES ABOUT COLLABORATIVE DECISION MAKING

There is an array of misgivings that people commonly express when efforts to change the methods of decision making are introduced. Employees are skeptical. They have seen this one before. "Oh sure," they say to themselves, "you are going to ask for my input. I'll bet you have your mind made up before the conversation even starts." On the other side, managers are mistrustful: "You mean I'm just going to let them decide and then have to go along with their decision?!"

In essence, employees are worried that methods 3 or 4 are really a different version of method 1. Managers anticipate that methods 3 or 4 are the first step toward anarchy. These doubts are typical of the cynicism and worst-case thinking some employ as the discussion on decision making begins. In both cases we think the real source of anxiety is method 4. People are skeptical that it can really work. Because of previous bad experiences, some believe that it is impossible for individuals at different organizational levels to sit down together, thoroughly evaluate a problem, and come to a trustworthy agreement. Both managers and employees imagine that at some time it will come down to a matter of rank, and that rank, for better or worse, will prevail.

Collaborative decision making is therefore the skill we believe it is most necessary to acquire. Of all the decision-making methods, method 4 is the one that most directly results in a reduction of fear. As a group gets better at collaboration, members see that the leader is fallible and does not have all the right answers, yet does not pull rank. It is possible to work things through to consensus. The leader discovers that the group is rational and committed to a quality decision. It is not necessary to fear that members will force self-interested practices on the organization. The cycle of mistrust is overcome by method 4.

Developing these skills and the trust that goes along with them does not occur quickly. People may have operated for a long time in constricted settings where they believed that only methods 1, 2, or 3 were possible or right. By comparison, method 4 feels very new. They do not know if they can do it, or even if they want to do it. Method 4, after all, implies a level of partnership and responsibility that can change the whole fabric of their relationships with their peers, customers, and the boss. It changes the role of the leader. People's expectations about what they and the organization can do may be very low, and method 4 can feel like an incredible stretch. Method 5, for such beginning groups, is usually unthinkable.

THE ROLE OF THE LEADER

In general, we believe that managers, as leaders of the decision-making process, are responsible for the tasks in the following list. As groups move toward an increased proportion of methods 4 and 5, some of these tasks may be deemphasized or transferred to the group:

- Describing the various methods and the roles of people within each approach

- Starting the process by deciding which method should be used to make the decision and communicating with the group about the method

- Initially framing the question to be decided

- In methods 1–3, clarifying or communicating the decision once it has been made and explaining the reasoning behind the decision to others affected by it

The end result of performing these tasks is that the leader facilitates the development of the group. It is impossible for a group to move toward methods 4 and 5 without the members building their innate problem-solving and decision-making skills. The goal is to help people share in the problems of judgment and complexity that afflict many strategic and operational decisions. Instead of being responsible for tackling all the dilemmas yourself, share responsibility for them using method 4. This effort is the major tool with which to combat the fear caused by "secretive decision making."

When people have become skilled at collaborative problem solving, the following traits are typical:

- The group works from an agenda; it moves quickly from decision to decision as it addresses needed topics within a known but flexible time frame.

- There are numerous "process" comments, such as "How do the rest of you feel about this?" and "I think we are getting off on a tangent here," that encourage and manage communication; the leader is not the only person making these comments.

- People feel free to brainstorm informally, to throw new ideas or possibilities on the table rather than making formal pronouncements of opinion.

- There are high levels of interaction, usually accompanied by a balance of laughter and moments of serious exchange; everyone participates in a meaningful way.

- Objections, differing perspectives, and disagreements are welcomed as a way to ensure quality outcomes.

- There is no sense that any one person's ideas dominate or that someone's private "agenda" has been forced on the group.

- There is a noncompetitive environment in which people ask for feedback and ideas from one another.

- People show a willingness to reflect on how the team is operating and how decisions are being made in order to improve the group process.

- The group has a high sense of accomplishment and achievement.

The following suggestions can help you and your group approach this goal. Initially the strategies concentrate on examining and cleaning up the current process. These techniques lay the groundwork for collaboration. Without them groups can easily confuse the decision they are trying to make with the process they are trying to follow. While some of these techniques may seem very elementary, they may be the very things groups need to reduce ambiguity and tension. They are often things people know they should do but do not take time to include. In such situations, we have usually found that decision-making processes are taken for granted and are correspondingly sloppy. Embarking on a "back to basics" approach frees the group to employ less structured methods in the future. When the process is not working, you and the group can drop back to a familiar technique to get past the barriers. Later in the chapter, we focus on more specific facets of collaboration.

BECOMING AWARE OF CURRENT DECISION-MAKING PATTERNS

If you want to improve your decision making, you need to become aware of your current patterns before you can plan the changes you want and need to make.

Consider Your Own Preferences About Decision Making

Give consideration to your role as someone who supervises and is supervised. As you respond to the following questions, see if there are themes that emerge from your answers.

As a manager of others, and as an employee:

- Which type of decision making makes you most comfortable?

- Which type do you prefer—intellectually, practically, and emotionally?
- What benefits and detriments are associated with each type?
- When would you be most inclined to use each type?
- What evidence do you find that people regard the decision-making methods of managers and supervisors as secretive or otherwise suspect?

As an employee:

- What assumptions do you make about your boss and his or her ability to make sound decisions?
- When do you distrust or feel left out of decisions?
- What impact does this have on your productivity or the quality of your work?
- Does it affect your willingness to speak up?
- Does it affect your willingness to help implement the decision?
- How often do you see your boss making decisions by method 1? method 2? method 3? method 4? method 5?

As a manager:

- How often do you see yourself making decisions by method 1? method 2? method 3? method 4? method 5?
- On what kinds of decisions would you be unwilling to use method 3? method 4? method 5? Why?
- What assumptions do you make about your employees and their ability to make sound decisions?
- How would you describe the decision-making process that is currently employed with your direct subordinates?
- How do you think they would describe it?
- How effective is your decision making? Where does it work? Where does it break down?

Ask People Who Work for You About Their Perceptions of Decision Making

Ask your staff about methods used, their effectiveness, and changes they would recommend. If you sense there is tension around this issue, bring in an outside person to do the interviewing and prepare a summary statement of what people say. Share the summary with your staff and discuss its implications. Make some agreements about ways to handle decision making more effectively in the future.

Make Decisions in Staff Meetings and Ask Someone to Observe

Ask your observer to pay particular attention to the way decisions are approached, discussed, and decided. Listen to his or her feedback and discuss its implications. Make decisions to eliminate current counterproductive practices. A finance department in a 5,000-person service organization asked for this type of assistance from us. We observed four senior-level staff meetings and presented a summary of our observations at the fifth. While the feedback addressed interpersonal communication as well as decision making, it was a catalyst for the group to decide to do a number of specific things to improve its process, including the following three items:

- When a person brings a decision to the group, the issue will be presented as a question focused on a particular action, for example: "Should we . . . ?" or "What should . . . ?"

- Each person responsible for bringing a decision to the group will announce if input from the group is desired (method 3) or if the group is to make the decision together (method 4).

- At each meeting, someone will be assigned to record decisions. When the meeting concludes, the list of decisions will be read to the group for verification and discussion of appropriate follow-up actions.

These are not complicated or original ideas. They are good techniques that help groups keep track of what they are deciding and how it is being decided. What makes them difficult is that implementing such agreements takes a willingness both to break old habits and, with some discipline, to establish new ones that are more productive.

SEEKING INPUT

If you do not want to make a decision alone, we suggest that you sidestep method 2 and opt at least for method 3. This requires some thought about who will be affected by the decision and how to gather at least a representative set of views from those individuals.

Think Carefully About the Method of Decision Making That Best Suits the Issue at Hand

Many leaders make the mistake of casually saying to a group something like this: "We need to make some decisions about budget priorities for the coming year. Tell me what you think." While that may represent a friendly way to get a group thinking about a set of concerns, it does not let people know the specific issue on which you want their views. Moreover, it suggests a level of involvement and participation that may be higher than the one you had in mind. You thought you implied method 3. Your group thought you implied method 4. The miscue on expectations is likely to cause trouble later.

Before Seeking Input from Individuals or a Group, Evaluate Your Question Critically

Ask yourself how the question will look and feel from others' perspectives. Does it make sense? Will people truly understand the kind of input you want? Are the words or concepts clear? For example, returning to the budget issue, there are varying levels of clarity:

Unclear	*" Tell me what you think about the budget priorities for next year. "*
Clearer	*" We are still undecided on next year's capital improvement budget. What do you think we ought to do with it? "*
Clearer still	*" Give me your yea or nay vote on each of the following items that fall into the capital improvement budget: two new cars for the auto pool, PCs for the marketing department, or refurbishing the lobby and customer service counter. "*

In refining a question related to decision making, it is not uncommon to rework the phrasing several times. Think about the information you really need to know. Is it data, experiences, feelings, predictions for the future, reactions to a past event, suggestions for improvements, or priorities?

Identify How Input Will Be Used—Who Will Make the Decision and How the Input Will Be Considered

For example, using method 3, you might say:

> 66 If you can get this to me by next Friday, I'll incorporate it into the information I'm getting from Ahmed, Barb, and Josh. I'll get a summary of responses back to all of you at our Tuesday staff meeting so that we can use that as a starting point for a method 3 discussion. I expect to use the ideas that come out of that discussion to make my recommendations to Terry by the end of the month. He's got the final say, but I expect him to go along with what we suggest. 99

Let People Know What Additional Information They Can Expect from You

It is important to inform people about follow-up, especially when they will hear about the final decision. For example,

> 66 Once I get my suggestions off to Terry, I'll send a copy to you. Unfortunately, there's not enough time for me to run this by anybody before I have to meet his deadline. I expect that he'll sign off on this request by a month from now. Once I know, I'll let you know. 99

PREPARING FOR COLLABORATION

As you move into group discussion settings, carefully attend to the problem-solving process. We suggest the following basic, structured approach:

1. Use an agenda. Meetings without them can drift intolerably. Know which areas are purely informational, which are discussion items, which require decisions. Review the agenda at the start of the meeting and allocate time as a group to each of the items. This will enable you to stay on track or make conscious decisions to deviate from your proposed sequence and time frame.

2. Keep tangents to a minimum. If they do come up, call them out. A good way to handle them is for one person to keep a list of the

tangential ideas that arise during the discussion. At the end of the meeting, review the list and decide how and when to handle each item on the list.

3. When you are brainstorming ideas, stick to the guidelines for encouraging creativity and participation. All too often brainstorming gets sloppy. After one or two ideas are suggested, someone will offer an evaluative comment. Someone else will jump in with another idea. Another person tosses in a tangential idea. Then the group has no idea what's happened. Focus on listing all the ideas with no comment. After about ten or fifteen minutes, shift to evaluating the ideas. When the evaluation is done and the merits of each idea have been discussed, call for the question.

4. When a decision has been made, have someone record it and read it back to the group. This does three things: It focuses people on what has actually been decided. It also gives them an opportunity to change any wording that might be misleading or unclear. Finally, the list serves as an important part of your meeting minutes.

5. Before your meeting ends, review what you have decided and agree on the next steps. Identify any follow-up actions, who will take the lead, and any necessary timelines. This too can go into the meeting's minutes and serve as a reminder when developing future agendas.

MOVING FROM PARTICIPATION TO COLLABORATION

The tools we have listed so far foster cooperative action and participation. They can help bring groups to the brink of the collaboration represented in method 4. To move to that next stage of development, you will need to lead the group into an examination of how it is working together to make decisions. This requires that you and the group together

- Define consensus decision making (what does method 4 really mean to people?)
- Identify norms for member participation
- Identify methods for handling problems in achieving consensus
- Examine your role and impact as the leader

Here are a few suggestions about how to proceed:

1. Clarify your intentions with the group to move toward a consensus-based approach for decisions. Emphasize your faith in the group's competence and skills. Identify your reasons for wanting to move in this direction—for example, your desire to help the group achieve even higher levels of teamwork or learn to wrestle with and work through business issues that you have been handling alone. Suggest that a first, concrete step is to have the group develop its own operational definition of consensus decision making.

2. Share the five-point model used in the first pages of this chapter. Ask the group to work through its own definition of method 4. Obviously, in itself this exercise is one of consensus building. The group should be encouraged to explore such topics as the difference between voting and consensus, the advantages and disadvantages of each, and particularly the level of agreement required of individuals to achieve consensus. As mentioned earlier, our own definition of consensus is "what we can agree to so we can move forward together." The focus is on action, on moving forward. This does not necessarily mean that each person is thrilled with, or even fully agrees with, the decision. It does mean that each person buys into the decision and will actively support its implementation.

Defining consensus can lead to a rich discussion of commitment and responsibility and of the complexities of day-to-day work as a member of a team. Members may ask, "So does this mean I can't change my mind?" "When can decisions legitimately be made outside the group?" or "How will this affect us as we work on our separate projects?" As the team responds to these questions, it is developing its group norms for decision making. These should be recorded and distributed to all members. From time to time, the norms should be evaluated and changed, if necessary.

WHAT IF CONSENSUS DOES NOT WORK?

A natural question at this stage is "What do we do if we can't come to consensus?" This is a vitally important question for the group to address. When groups cannot reach consensus they easily become dispirited or immobilized. People may back into finger pointing, or they may simply push decisions back onto the leader, rather than examining and dealing with the causes of the problem.

A group of managers we worked with ran into a stone wall when several members regularly sabotaged the consensus-building process. A small, powerful clique within the group continually raised questions and expressed doubts about the direction in which the group wanted to go. Other group members were generally uncomfortable dealing with conflict in a direct manner. They wanted everyone to be happy with each decision. This combination of counteracting forces prevented the group from making any decisions that stuck. What decisions were made were frequently reversed at a following meeting after one of the powerful few "had time to rethink the decision."

Situations like this one illustrate the internal barriers to quality decisions that may be brought to the surface as the possibility of consensus is explored. They are opportunities for the group to learn about its own dynamics and make plans to overcome problem behavior. Doing so is an important team-building accomplishment. Particularly as groups new to consensus decision making get started, it may feel as if the team is taking too long to get off the ground. Decisions may seem mired in windy, nonspecific discussions or may skirt the edges of undiscussable issues which could be "black holes."

At this stage people are learning. You can be helpful by keeping the conversation on track and providing reassurance that the group is doing a good job. Counsel patience. Some of this floundering is tolerable and even desirable because it means that the group is sorting out its own standards for problem solving and decision making. The group is not just talking about consensus building; it is living it, and it is working out what consensus means in terms of behavior, not only ideas. Once a group has worked through a few difficult decisions, it typically gets much faster in its approach.

Do not allow your group to flounder too long. From a practical standpoint, this means that decisions are not being made; in turn, this is liable to affect the confidence level of the team. Groups committed to collaborative decision making need to figure out what they will do if consensus cannot be reached. They need guidelines for what to do if they get stuck. When a group listens to all sides of a question and cannot come to agreement after several tries, you, or whoever is leading or facilitating the meeting, should make the observation: "We don't seem to be able to reach consensus. How shall we handle this?" The aim is to create a safe environment in which to look at whatever is getting in the way. In the case of the difficult situation cited in this section, the problem was complex and emotional and required outside intervention. The group had a hard time facing the reasons it had become stuck. In other cases, the barrier may be momentary or situational.

Voting may be the simplest method of overcoming the hurdle, although a group might well have other proposals. For voting, usually a specific majority count—such as two-thirds or three-quarters—is established ahead of time. If the group decides that it cannot decide through consensus, and it is time to make a decision, then a vote can be taken. Another common backup plan is for the decision to revert to method 3 and for you, as leader, to then make it. If patterns in the use of these backup methods occur, or if they are used too frequently, it is a sign that the group needs to evaluate its process and its barriers to reaching consensus.

THE IMPACT OF THE LEADER

A tricky aspect of collaborative decision making is how to arrange things so the leader can be "just plain folks" during the decision-making process. Assigning a group member other than the leader to be the facilitator, or bringing in someone from the outside to play that part, can be a great help. If that is not possible, the leader needs to wear two hats at once. In this case, we advise leaders to do what is necessary to develop their group facilitation skills. Tips include:

- Hold your comments until several others have spoken. If you jump in right away, you may unnecessarily sway the group.

- Use your listening skills. Paraphrase what you hear others say—especially before you disagree with them.

- If you find yourself needing to speak as the leader, announce that you are doing so. Code phrases sometimes help to lighten this action—for example: "Let me put on my department manager hat for a minute . . ."

- At the end of a decision-making session, ask the group for feedback: Did you dominate? If so, how did that happen? Did people have a sense that you were in the decision as an equal? What could you do next time to increase the sense of collaboration in the group?

The ultimate goal of this work is to develop an environment where no one is worried about your role. An example of this might be a situation in which people feel free enough to ask openly that you save your ideas until all members of the group have had a chance to express their views. Once such trust is established, it is possible to imagine a time when you and the team are operating so effectively that no one would worry about when you offer your input.

COMMUNICATING ABOUT DECISIONS THAT HAVE BEEN MADE

Many well-intentioned, collaborative leaders fail to take this one final and relatively simple step. They therefore perpetuate the impression that they are autocratic or secretive decision makers. This is especially true when a decision has been made by methods 1, 2, or 3.

At methods 4 and 5 the group takes on a significant role in communicating its actions. The same guidelines apply, however, and the team should not fail to create a communication plan for informing others whenever it makes decisions. As decisions are made by the group, some time should also be devoted to this plan. If it is not, the group will soon be perceived as a "closed club" and will look just as autocratic or secretive as the noncommunicative manager. Management teams which are internally very collaborative can easily fall into this trap.

Once a method 1, 2, or 3 decision has been made, make sure you communicate the decision as quickly as possible to those who were involved and those who will be affected by the outcomes. Highlight the options you considered and the reasons you selected your course of action. Also, it is important to review why you chose the method you used, particularly if you are talking to people who will be affected but who have not been involved in the decision-making process. This will help your communication come across as an explanation rather than a pronouncement.

If the input you received is not reflected in the decision, make sure you address that discrepancy. This is a most important step to take. It demonstrates that you truly heard the input and that you considered it. If you do not talk about this, people who offered input that is not reflected in your decision are likely to

- Assume that you had your mind made up to begin with
- Feel cheated because you wasted their time by asking for their input
- Mistrust you in the future when you ask for input

In this follow-up discussion, also mention any timelines associated with the implementation of the decision. Let people know what they can expect to see and when. If there will be opportunities in the future for them to be involved in implementing the decisions, describe these opportunities in as much detail as possible.

There is obviously a big difference between making a sound decision and effective decision-making processes. It is certainly possible for a lovely process to produce a lousy decision. However, we believe that under most circumstances, carefully considered decision-making processes will result in better business decisions. The suggestions made in this chapter are well tested. They have made an enormous difference in people's reactions to decisions that were made in work groups. In several situations we know well, building the skills and agreements that support collaborative decision making has represented one very tangible way to turn an environment of mistrust and fear into one of enthusiasm, creativity, and commitment.

15

CHALLENGE WORST-CASE THINKING

Worst-case thinking is "catastrophizing." A direct descendent of the cycle of mistrust, worst-case thinking is a nasty mind-trap that darkens people's attitudes and buries their ability to solve problems. It leads people into black-and-white dichotomous thinking that limits their capacity to manage the future.

Frequently obscured by the voices of "realism" or "pragmatism," worst-case

---

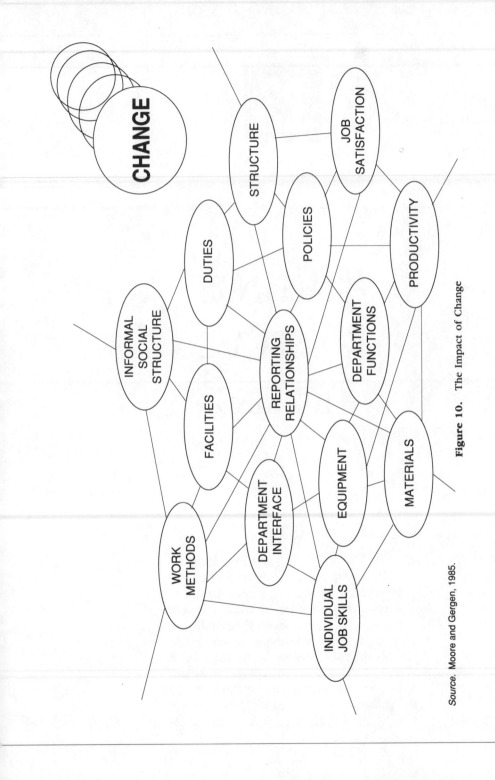

Figure 10. The Impact of Change

thinking snares most people at one time or another. If you listen closely, you can hear it from managers and employees alike. Some statements are more obvious than others:

> 66 *I would never dream of telling her that! She'd just blow up!* 99

> 66 *We can't just have people making those decisions on their own. If we don't have a senior management representative on that task force, who knows where they'll end up?* 99

> 66 *This whole program is going down the tubes. I'll probably get fired—and get my boss fired, as well.* 99

> 66 *This employee committee is a setup. Do you think anybody is going to seriously consider our suggestions? There's only one person who makes decisions around here, and you know who I'm talking about.* 99

> 66 *I wouldn't be surprised if all these delays around the budget mean that there will be another bunch of layoffs.* 99

WORST-CASE THINKING IS TIED TO CHANGE

Throughout our research and consulting, we have repeatedly observed how easily people can become trapped by their negative assumptions. The worst case is a way of thinking that happens so naturally and usually so fast that people hardly notice. This is especially true during times of change.

Maggie Moore and Paul Gergen, consultants with a specialty in risk taking and change, have developed a model we find particularly useful. Their model, shown in Figure 10, explains the reasons why during times of change more people are likely to be affected by worst-case thinking. They suggest that when people are bombarded by a change outside their control, the impact is likely to be felt in many different ways. Their model shows how a change, such as the introduction of a new production line, a layoff, or a job reclassification, can operate like a fast-moving, powerful object descending on a web of interconnected aspects of organizational life.

For example, new safety regulations mandated by the government might influence what clothes employees wear to work, how many people and how long it takes to complete a job, or what work methods are used. In turn, these apparently small adjustments may influence training and workloads or cause a shift in working relationships and social structure, perhaps including the informal rules of the work group about safety matters. These changes, some obvious and some not, travel through the net shown in Figure 10. The bigger the change and the faster it happens, the greater the number of areas that will be affected. All of this begins to accumulate as an *emotional* impact on those influenced by the change.

We would add that as more elements of the net are affected, more people have opportunities for worst-case thinking and for personalizing how the change could negatively affect them. In the scenario we have just created, employees may begin to see a significant loss of freedom or wonder if management will use the new rules to penalize them in some way. To carry out this worst-case imagining, some may worry that management will give the rules as a reason to grant smaller pay increases due to the cost of implementing the new regulations. In turn, this might cause some to be concerned about their individual finances and other personal issues.

"Nothing's as sure as change" does not offer much solace to the individuals or work group grappling with unknown possibilities that might significantly alter the quality of their work and work life. It is tough enough in organizations where information flows quickly and freely, where managers and employees have a history of planning and working together to solve problems. It is doubly difficult in settings where the cycle of mistrust dominates boss-employee relations and hierarchical traditions limit employee access to information and involvement in decision making.

Being stuck in an either-or mentality keeps individuals from thinking rationally. It prevents them from successfully collaborating on a plan to manage the change. It certainly keeps them from planning what they might do in the event that the worst case actually happens. In such situations, they are also unable to anticipate the events that are most likely to happen. As one technical writer from a manufacturing plant in western New York described it, "It's like crashing and burning." He agreed with the CEO from Atlanta who suggested:

> 66 *Nine out of ten will assume the worst. When their security is threatened, people don't take risks because of fear of failure, fear of not knowing what to do. If you can answer the 'What then?' question comfortably, you become better able to handle the changes.* 99

Worst-case thinking positions people to be more likely to be threatened by ambiguous behaviors. For this reason, the cycle of mistrust described in Chapter Seven is particularly hard to reverse. This makes it easier to understand why some people have such a hard time with change—even in a world where change is a constant factor.

For these reasons, we devote this chapter to suggestions that encourage people to name their worst fears and, as calmly as possible, to figure out ways to deal with them. We believe that once these fears can be named and said out loud, their power will diminish significantly. To assist with this reversal, we suggest identifying and planning for *both* the worst case and the most likely case. First, however, we offer clues that will help you to know when your employees have slipped into the crash-and-burn frame of mind and ways to assist them back onto a more reasonable course. Our suggestions in this first part of the chapter emphasize the individual employee's emotions and the pragmatic, one-on-one coaching role you might play. This is appropriate because of the sensitive, personal qualities of worst-case thinking that people sometimes express.

HOW TO RECOGNIZE WORST-CASE THINKING

Worst-case thinking can happen to anybody, even very positive and rational people. In this section we suggest what to look for in others' behavior which may indicate that worst-case thinking has taken hold. We also offer a description of what it feels like to be caught in these negative, either-or patterns. As you read through this material, try to recall the last time you found yourself in this thinking mode. As with most of the dynamics we discuss in this book, the better you understand your own related experience, the more able you will be to assist others.

What People Experience with Worst-Case Thinking

Worst-case thinking is like unexpectedly breaking through the ice of a frozen pond. In an instant, fear-oriented thinking takes over. People recognize that they are at risk. But instead of figuring out what to do to correct the situation, they frequently become immobilized and panic, unable to think clearly in the frigid water.

People imagining the worst case lose their ability to see a range of options for future actions. When work problems crop up, some picture a riches-to-rags scenario: Successful person with healthy, happy relationships ends up jobless, friendless, and homeless. For others it is the nightmare about missing the final college exam come true: "At last," they think, "everyone will find out how incompetent and ignorant I really am!"

Strong emotions can be present and are frequently expressed in the form of anxious, panicked requests for assistance. People typically feel unable to turn this downward spiral around and see correcting the situation about as likely as stopping a moving freight train. While others may be helpful and have good ideas, it feels to the person involved as if the only possible remedy is some type of divine intervention, a made-in-Hollywood ending that comes out of nowhere to save the day. When they are caught in this pattern, people are obviously not thinking rationally.

Clues to Worst-Case Thinking

There are observable signs that often accompany worst-case thinking. Some are related to statements people make. Others are more nonverbal in nature. These are all relative, depending on the normal disposition, communication, and problem-solving style a person usually demonstrates. The actual signs may vary from one person to another. However, each indicates a significant movement toward a more negative perspective.

Frequently, the first clues are comments that express clear, but not extreme, discouragement, cynicism, frustration, or fear. Examples include:

> 66 *I'm just not sure this is going to work.* 99

> 66 *I don't think we've looked at all the risks.* 99

> 66 *I am beginning to wonder where all this is going.* 99

> 66 *If we don't pull this off, we're going to be in deep trouble.* 99

> 66 *I don't understand what this whole thing is about, anyway.* 99

If you respond to such an opening statement with something as simple as "Oh? What do you mean?" you will most likely hear and see additional signs, such as

- Statements predicting impending disaster
- Acknowledgment of only two options: good or bad with nothing in between
- Strong expressions of cynicism, powerlessness, mistrust, and fear
- Agitation or inability to concentrate on constructive problem solving

When these signs are visible, we encourage you to slow down and put yourself into the role of listener and clarifier. By asking simple questions and applying your good listening skills in a supportive, attentive way, you can be very helpful. Remember that no matter how unlikely someone's worst case seems to you, it is a very serious matter to that person. If you become judgmental or switch into a managerial "fix-it" mode, you will not be effective. Avoid phrases such as

❝ *Don't be ridiculous. That's never going to happen.* ❞

❝ *Oh, that's really easy, all you have to do is . . .* ❞

❝ *Well, you got yourself into this. I guess you better get yourself out.* ❞

Words like these will only cause the person you want to help to feel more isolated in his or her worries.

IDENTIFYING THE WORST CASE AND THE MOST LIKELY CASE

When they are trapped by worst-case thinking, people frequently cannot even voice what they are worried about. It can be of great assistance to simply help them articulate the fate that might befall them. Exploring imagined worst-case scenarios enables people to let go of a significant amount of emotional tension. When this happens, it is possible to engage them in a discussion of what is most *likely* to happen. This more reality-focused view creates a platform for eventual planning and problem solving.

In your discussion, ask simple questions and apply your listening skills in an attentive, caring way. Our first suggestion is more direct and is best used in one-on-one situations with someone to whom you can comfortably give straightforward feedback. The other approaches are more oblique and work very well with people who are linear in their thinking style and who are not at ease with discussions about feelings.

Ask If a Person Is Getting Caught Up into Worst-Case Thinking

When you hear or see any of the clues described in the previous section, simply ask the person in a caring tone, "Are you getting caught up in worst-case thinking?" The typical response will be, "What do you mean?" Offer an observation such as "You just seem to be so convinced that everything will turn out badly. I'm concerned that you are limiting your options and assuming only the worst will happen." Such an introduction usually triggers a short discussion where the other person explains what is going on and why he or she feels scared or stuck.

During the conversation, your role is to listen and reflect back what you hear. A straightforward sequence may be helpful:

- First focus on the emotional side, acknowledging the feelings that you hear.

- When the time seems right to shift gears, explore the other person's picture of the worst case.

- Then move the discussion into a problem-solving phase where the emphasis is on what can be done to prevent the worst case from happening and to handle it if it does occur.

- When you have finished talking about the worst case, explore the other person's sense of what the most likely scenario will be and how she or he feels about that possibility.

Throughout the conversation, be ready to shift your attention back to focus on feelings. If there is something tangible that you can do to help, offer to do it. Often a small step, like making a phone call or getting a piece of information, will loosen up the other person's ability to act. It is a symbolic gesture, in part, where you figuratively take someone by the arm and through your offer of help say, "Come on, let's get started."

Obviously, as with other discussions of undiscussables, you may be opening up bigger issues than you imagined. Do not get trapped—or trap yourself—into the role of therapist or counselor. The formula we have just provided works well for work-related issues and concerns, such as a particularly difficult work assignment. But we know from experience that self-esteem issues can also surface that may be far beyond the range of a manager's coaching role. If the conversation repeatedly returns to the employee's private view of personal deficits and lasts more than an hour or so, it is time to make a referral to an agency or employee assistance program. You will do the employee a major disservice by getting hooked into the role of amateur psychologist.

Ask People What Could Go Wrong

A very practical and acceptable activity with any group or individual grappling with some kind of change is to ask, "What could go wrong?" All kinds of answers can follow, ranging from personal to systems issues. Such a discussion can set the stage for you to ask three additional questions:

> 66 *What's the worst thing that could happen throughout all this?* 99

> 66 *What's the most likely scenario?* 99

> 66 *What do you think we need to do in order to make this be as successful as possible?* 99

Asking these questions does not have to be a big deal. The sequence is important, however, because it enables people to talk about their fears within the context of a problem-solving discussion. For those who are uncomfortable talking about their feelings, and especially their fears, in a business setting, this approach allows them an acceptable, logical way to talk about their opinions, values, and emotions. The last question positions the individual or the group for action. Having a plan of action usually helps people to feel better about the unknown.

Ask People How They Are Doing

If you pay attention to the people who are most affected by changes, you may notice that one or two seem to be having a hard time. Their sense of humor may have disappeared and their concentration may have slipped. Attendance or tardiness may have become an issue. The quality of their work or their productivity may have fallen off. If you see those clues, ask people how they are doing. Listen carefully to what they say. Depending on the relationship you have with a person and his or her willingness to be confronted, apply either of the two approaches we have just described.

Identify Hopes, Fears, and Expectations

Hopes, fears and expectations can be explored in one-on-one situations as in the previous three suggestions. Posing these same topics for a group, however, can generate an illuminating and energizing discussion.

A consulting experience of a colleague illustrates the use of this technique. The method was used with a group of fifteen senior managers in an organization charged with putting on a major international event. Five months before the event, many of these executives were still quite nervous about how the logistics were actually going to come together. In the early part of an all-day retreat, the consultant asked people, in groups of two and three, to talk through their thoughts about the next five months. They were asked to describe their hopes about how the event would come together. Next, they were asked to describe their fears regarding the same issue. Those answers were eventually reported to the group as a whole. Some of the fears that were identified included the following concerns:

- Senior managers would not be able to perform under pressure.

- Lack of clarity about the budget issues would be a problem and would prevent people from spending the resources that were actually available.

- The organization would avoid making difficult or sensitive decisions until it was too late.

Once the hopes and fears had been listed for the group, people engaged in a discussion of their actual expectations. The consultant then drew a continuum with the hopes represented at one end and the fears at the other. He asked people, one by one, to tell their colleagues in which spot on the continuum their own set of expectations fell, with the results as shown in Figure 11. As a group, their expectations were much closer to their hopes than to their fears. To them, this was a pleasant and surprising revelation.

The consultant applied this exercise on the spot because he saw that many negatives were coming up and he wanted to provide a balanced structure for people to use while they were thinking about their concerns. He also wanted this group of high-task, hard-driving

Hopes									Fears
x	x								
x	x	x							
x	x x x	x			x				
1	2	3	4	5	6	7	8	9	10

Figure 11. Actual Hopes and Fears

senior-level people to think about their feelings and articulate them to their peers. This all took about an hour and a half and enabled people to move through the day with their worst fears openly discussed.

BUILDING PLANS OF ACTION FOR EACH CASE

When people manage their worst-case thinking, they recognize it when it happens and move on. They do not get stuck. They have a plan and know when to implement it. This readiness inspires additional confidence which, in turn, reduces the presence of fear.

Develop Criteria to Identify When the Worst Case Is About to Happen

As with all the other suggestions in this chapter, this strategy is designed to get people to slow down and apply some logic to their fears. It also enables them to know what to look for as indicators that the worst case has arrived.

Once again, start by asking simple questions: "How will you know when the worst case has arrived?" "What will happen?" Answers might include the following situations:

- The budget is reduced another 3 percent.
- Good people start leaving of their own accord.
- When they do, no one is hired to replace them.
- Key programs are cut.
- I'm asked to change jobs and work for Bart (who I can't stand).

Lists like this one become yardsticks against which individuals can measure their fears. Until the criteria are met, the individual will know that events are still moving at an acceptable level. When the early warning signs start to appear, individuals will know when to put their action plans into operation. As a manager or peer, once you know the criteria, you will be in a better position to provide support or guidance if the worst case does come along.

Develop a Plan

While it is certainly possible to work individually with people to help them develop a plan to manage the worst case, we suggest that this happen in a group. Often the fears experienced by one person are shared by others, especially if they concern upcoming changes or an ambiguous organizational future. In such cases, it makes sense to invite those who will be affected by the change to participate. If the fears are truly limited to one person, asking one or two others to serve as consultants can add to the quality of the planning and will let the worst-case thinker know that others are ready to help.

Once the worst and most likely cases have been identified, it is time to pose some key planning questions:

- What can be done to prevent the worst case from happening?
- What events do we control or have influence over?
- What events do we need to be ready to accept?
- What can be done to help people get ready to handle the worst case if and when it comes?
- If it comes, what can be done to make the situation less troublesome, threatening, confusing, or frustrating?
- What other options exist for people who cannot manage the worst case?

It is probably best if small groups of people tackle these questions. There is strength in numbers, especially for individuals who might be feeling worried or tense about possible events. If a large group is involved, the ideas which come from the small groups can be reported on for large-group discussion.

It is also important to remember that taking action on any of the answers to these questions may be hard for some people. If they have become accustomed to a dependent pattern of behavior, taking action to get ready for difficulty or prevent it from happening will represent a major shift. Seeing you or other co-workers acting on the collaboratively designed plans will give these individuals extra encouragement to take action of their own.

One of the organizations we visited had recently gone through a restructuring. A senior vice-president reflected on the way it was "sprung," in spite of how "we preach partnership and collegiality." He noted that the "change has destroyed the emotional links people had with the organization. People now worry about when the next shoe will drop." Another senior vice-president added that although many people are now beginning to see the benefits for the organization, "there is one officer a week going to see the employee assistance program folks." He acknowledged that these mid-level career employees had to be thinking about what the reorganization meant for their careers and their families.

It is exactly this type of environment where worst-case thinking needs to be managed most carefully. When many people are waiting for shoes to drop, they will understandably be inclined toward skeptical, cynical, and fearful thinking. The idea behind this strategy is that helping people to name and then listen to their worst-case fears helps them to shape a more positive reality. This happens because people feel attended to, respected, and accepted. The process enables them to take a more realistic view and positions them to be more effective problem solvers and contributors.

PART FOUR

■

CONCLUSION:
CREATING A
QUALITY
ORGANIZATION

16

PEOPLE ARE READY FOR A WORKPLACE WITHOUT FEAR

In this final chapter, we celebrate managers who intuitively understand and are committed to reducing fear. In bringing closure to this discussion of fear in the workplace, we offer two additional elements: ideas on how to extend the work of reducing fear beyond the individuals who report to you and a summary of the challenges you will face as you pursue this goal. This last chapter blends a few final practical suggestions with a return to the vision of a quality organization. Like climbers, we keep one hand on the rock while another searches for a higher hold.

With most of the action steps thus far suggested, we have focused on the world of the manager and that person's direct subordinates. We have done this intentionally, believing that unless fear can be reduced within one's primary work team, it probably will not be influenced in the broader organization. We also sense that, depending on how high up that primary work team is in the hierarchy, changes there may make a great difference for many other people.

The steps beyond these strategies move out from the work team in every direction. They are based on the notion that one person alone cannot reduce fear in the organization. They offer additional contexts for leadership with subordinates, peers, and your supervisor—some of which may be even more challenging than the tasks we have thus far described. Each of these areas is worth a book of its own.

ADDITIONAL STEPS WITH YOUR WORK TEAM

Given that a manager and his or her work team are a relatively small part of the whole, there is a real necessity to move the awareness of fear and the commitment to operating in new ways down the organization. This can best be accomplished if the team of people who report to you trust one another. The team can then act in concert to reduce fear within the organization.

It is self-evident that the work of reducing fear must include diminishing mistrust *among* your direct subordinates. The dependency that plagues hierarchy will not be truly overcome until the focus changes from the way team members respond to you to the way they respond to one another. As a leader, your role is to help the team work together, not just to improve how it works with you.

The following suggestions often are best carried out with the assistance of an outside facilitator or consultant. This can help you to give your team the freedom and responsibility to solve its own problems. It allows you to subtly shift in your role toward being an empowering guide, supporter, and mentor to the group.

Use a Variety of Team-Building Techniques to Improve Relations Among Your Subordinates

Some approaches to this task include

- Development of a shared vision and purpose; creation of long- and short-range plans
- Clear agreements around communication, decision making, and conflict management
- Clarification of individual roles, authority, and accountability
- Sorting through specific interpersonal conflicts
- Setting aside time to learn and apply quality-improvement methods and tackling process issues which affect the team

Help team members "discuss the undiscussables" with one another.   These undiscussables may relate to

- Unresolved conflicts
- Misunderstandings
- Common problems which have not been given sufficient time and attention
- The performance level of team members

Teams that cannot talk about their undiscussables are almost certainly doomed to a static world of mediocre communication and suboptimal performance. They will ultimately be dependent on their leader for direction and inspiration. Unfortunately, both managers and employees may have so thoroughly accepted traditional functioning that they have a hard time conceiving of a team that functions around the core behaviors described in Chapter Eight. Moving in this direction can involve training in specific interpersonal skills for team members and close work with a consultant or facilitator. The cautions listed in Chapter Thirteen, "Discuss the Undiscussables," should be heeded.

Collaboratively make plans as a team to move fear-reduction strategies lower in the organization.   The best outcomes result when members, as a group, understand and freely adopt the challenge of reducing fear. Members of your team can operate as a support network for one another as they initiate efforts with their own subordinates. Even if the group cannot reach consensus, this should not prevent individual subordinate managers from applying the concepts to their work areas. Before proceeding with any formal effort to reduce fear, the group should carefully evaluate how to manage change in the organization, who else needs to be involved in the decision, and how that decision can best be communicated.

REDUCING FEAR WITH PEERS

Extending the effort to reduce fear among your peers is important work because lateral mistrust—particularly at the middle and upper layers of the hierarchy—can have a devastating impact on the way the rest of the organization operates. Others at lower levels are likely to feel caught up in the conflict and the ambiguities at higher levels.

One human resources director for a major corporation told us that he believed peers at the top may have even more at stake in their relations with one another than they do in their relations with the boss. His point reinforced our belief that the cycle of mistrust can easily be applied to peer relations. Negative assumptions about peers are self-reinforcing and also can feed a general environment of mistrust in the organization.

Initiate Improvements in Relations with Your Peers

Don't wait for improvements. Too frequently, people are unwilling to take the first steps toward understanding and managing their conflicts. They wait for the other person to bring forward evidence of good faith and trustworthiness. This effectively maintains the status quo. Good ways to initiate improvements include:

- Asking for and offering feedback about the relationship
- Asking another party to facilitate or mediate a discussion of differences between yourself and a co-worker
- Tactfully discussing undiscussables in one-on-one meetings
- Collaborating on operational projects of mutual benefit
- Talking openly with peers about your values and your desire to reduce competition by developing a more collaborative work environment for everyone

- Asking a peer to serve as a sounding board for you on a problem
- Calling out worst-case thinking or the cycle of mistrust when you see it among your peer group

Share Information with Your Peers

When it is appropriate, share information with your peers about your efforts to reduce fear within the team of people who report to you. Being open about this work may awaken an interest by others in addressing similar needs. It also models discussing the relationship side of work. This may create opportunities for additional disclosure and trust building with your peers.

REDUCING FEAR WITH YOUR SUPERVISOR

We have resisted addressing this topic at length in this book because of our firm belief that the primary responsibility of managers is to reduce fear with those lower in the hierarchy. Working in the opposite direction, no matter how tempting, is a secondary consideration. However, we also know that many managers will feel that fear generated higher in the organization can only undermine their own efforts. And, frankly, it can be personally very stressful if you believe you are working for a Darth Vader. Some of the steps we suggest will depend a great deal on the level of interpersonal risk you are willing to absorb. Know what the stakes are before proceeding.

Check Your Own Cycle of Mistrust

Are you making negative assumptions or attributions of motive based on limited information? Is your sense of risk the result of threatening behavior, does it have the flavor of worst-case imagining, or is it a combination of the two? Do your best to sort out behavior from interpretation and grant the benefit of the doubt whenever possible.

Ask For and Offer Feedback

As with your peers, you may be the person who needs to take the first step. Do not make the assumption that your boss "won't listen anyway." Tactfully presented information about specific fear-provoking actions or behaviors can generate great credibility and respect. This is especially so when the feedback does not make assumptions, but focuses on effects. Accept a certain amount of defensiveness without getting "blown away." Identify specific alternative behaviors with statements such as "What I believe might work better would be . . ." Be clear, factual, and straightforward about what you want. If you believe it will help, spend a few minutes explaining the cycle of mistrust so that there is a context for your comments.

Plant Seeds

Adapt the strategies in this book to your relationship with your boss. Describe the concepts of undiscussable issues or worst-case thinking. Identify what you believe are symptoms of fear in the organization. Talk about your own vision of a quality organization. Share a copy of this book and offer to discuss over lunch how you believe it applies to your organization. Talk about what you are doing to reduce fear within your own work areas and what the payoffs and benefits of doing so have been.

Learn to Cope or Find a Way to Leave

The time frame for creating change higher up in the system may be very long. You will need to decide whether you are willing to sustain that time frame or whether you should move on to other opportunities. Some situations are simply unchangeable, and spending the rest of your career trying to influence a stone wall may be a terrible waste of energy, time, and talent. Find a friend or career counselor to listen to you and help sort out options.

If you feel you cannot change the situation and also cannot leave, you will need to find ways to cope. This means maintaining perspective and not allowing the situation to affect your confidence, motivation, and commitment to quality work. If they are continually in jeopardy, you risk burnout. Again, find a trusted friend or helper to counsel with you about a personalized strategy. By all means do not become trapped by the feeling that you have to change the situation or others in order to maintain your self-esteem.

Extending the work of reducing fear beyond your immediate team means that you are operating as an agent of change in your organization, whether you are working with your employees, with peers, or with the person you report to. There are four additional pieces of advice we can provide to managers who see themselves as facilitators of workplace transformations:

1. Remember that reversing historic patterns of mistrust will not happen overnight. To use consultant Michael Doyle's phrase, you need to "go slow to go fast." Incremental change is frustrating and seems to take forever in the best of circumstances, but that is the way trust is established. This can be particularly hard for managers who are tuned to a fast pace. But as we have tried to convey many times, rushing forward inevitably causes people to stumble.

2. Don't get discouraged. As a manager friend of ours remarked, "Things in the middle always feel like they are failing." Maintaining an even and persistent approach in spite of setbacks has great power. The setbacks, in fact, may be important clues to where people really are in terms of their skills, values, and beliefs. Adapt as you proceed, and do not give up.

3. From Marvin Weisbord, we have learned the importance of focusing on a particular business aspect or opportunity that would be improved if fear were reduced (1987). For example, a reorganization or other new programs usually cause some fear. Applying the fear-reducing strategies to the achievement of a specific business objective helps people see how fear directly affects the work of the organization. It gives concreteness to the effort, and learning is likely to transfer to other contexts.

4. Finally, following the advice of Herb Shepard (1975), avoid "working uphill." Choose strategies and work in arenas where you will realize some success, where people will begin to notice a difference and feel good about what is happening. Do not try to do everything at once or to do the toughest things first.

CHALLENGES OF THE PATH

Those of us who are committed to the work of reducing fear often feel caught between the vision of the quality organization and reality. To use the phrase of one manager who believes in these ideals, we operate somewhere in the "gray spaces between what ought to be and what can be." The challenge of this work is felt constantly in the tension between our values and the nature of the organizations in which we operate.

W. Edwards Deming tells those who attend his seminars, "We are here to make another kind of world." He expresses the broad scope of the goal, and its enormity. Surely, the 1990s will be a decade when great progress toward this new kind of world will be made. Through focusing on customer requirements, the application of systems and statistical thinking, and the involvement of employees, organizations will follow the challenging path of transformation. Increasingly, organizational leaders are seeking information, experimenting, and learning how to change that fragment of the world where their influence counts the most.

Deming's words also mean that the challenge of improvement is not one to be lightly considered. Managers who lead their organizations know what it is like to be vulnerable: not to have the right answer, to know there probably *is* no single right answer, and to address the emotional side of business, along with the linear and logical side. Looking at the fear in an organization and investigating its causes can be a journey toward an awesome starting point where the hard work of transformation becomes clear.

To achieve another kind of world requires a deep understanding of where we are now. The awareness of fear can help us move to this point. In the same way that many organizations have had to face harsh news about waste, scrap, and rework within their production processes, there is also harsh news about fear in human interactions in the workplace. But once past the denial that is so common, the real possibilities begin to emerge. When managers accept the role of facilitator, coach, and consultant, a dramatic shift takes place. Traditional notions of controlling and telling give way to inviting and guiding. Commitment switches to the long term—to the development of quality products and services, to long-lasting, mutually satisfying relationships with customers, vendors, and employees.

This challenge requires the leadership of managers and executives who are willing to do things differently, making both personal and organizational changes. It demands men and women who are willing to admit and learn from their mistakes, to seek involvement from people throughout their organizations, and to work hard in order to eliminate the technical and human barriers which prevent good ideas from happening. The challenge will be especially hard for those who have envisioned positions of organizational leadership as ones of unquestioned status and authority. Managers who do not want surprises and hate to hear bad news will have a tough time. People who are unwilling to seek and listen to personalized feedback are also likely to encounter many problems.

PEOPLE ARE READY

This book has been written for the managers who constantly probe those uneasy gray spaces between their values and their realities, wanting to push farther toward their vision in everything they do. There are a lot of people—managers and employees—who are doing their utmost to achieve a quality organization. One of the executives we know who best exemplifies this spirit is a man we will refer to here as Paul. At forty-one, he is president and CEO of a service organization owned by a much larger corporation. The fact that he has requested us not to use his real name says a lot about the tradeoffs he makes on a daily basis.

Paul was recruited away from a competitor four years ago to be the CEO of a company $1.5 million in the red. Within eighteen months, his organization broke even. For 1988–89, net income was at $2 million and "President" was added to his title. In the last two years, his organization has grown from $35 million to $75 million. These numbers describe him, in part: intelligent, savvy, and producing results in an incredibly competitive environment.

Those who report to Paul describe his leadership style as "bringing out the best in those who work for him." He sees himself as a facilitator —someone who secures the resources and provides the necessary consultation so that others can do their jobs. When asked about the most satisfying aspects of his work, he refers to times "when a group of us have worked on a problem and come to a solution that we all buy into. Then we do it." He adds, "I don't get my jollies from reading the month's profit and loss statements."

Success has involved more than hard work and long hours. The corporate environment that surrounds Paul's company is frequently characterized by fear. He spends a large percentage of his time buffering those who report to him from the bureaucratic, high-control practices of the parent organization. He knows that he was hired to turn his company around financially. He has done this through decentralized decision making, flexibility, high involvement with customers, and healthy doses of fun.

Sadly, the more successful his organization is, the greater resistance he and his employees experience from the corporation. On his last performance appraisal, he received a mediocre rating. He was told that his consensus style causes him "not to be objective" about those who report to him. His corporate superiors expressed concern that he was creating too much of a "family" atmosphere.

However, Paul is unyieldingly optimistic about the future. He believes firmly that we are on the verge of a dramatic change in the way organizations operate. In the last ten years, he says,

> ❝ Many of us have been trained and facilitated to death. And I mean that positively. We've learned about the importance of communication, honesty, quality, and integrity. But the content of the training does not match the way we do business. We are working in systems that do not enable us to put these positive ideas into practice.
>
> ❝ All the recent changes in the world make it seem like anything is possible. When the baton gets passed, things will change quickly. The possibilities will be endless. ❞

Paul indicts those in key positions who "think they're different than front-line workers." From his point of view, the "hopes, dreams, and desires of the employee on the front line are the same as those of the people at the top. The problem is leadership, not people. People are ready." What the workplace is ready for, he continues, is leadership that truly supports people, "the kind of leadership described by Peters and Waterman and Bennis and Weisbord. It feels right, it sounds right, and in their hearts, people know it is right."

When this style of leadership is not reinforced by those at the top, it creates Paul's greatest source of impatience: "a whole organization full of bright, well-trained, thoughtful people ready to do extraordinary things" who are blocked by practices and beliefs that are based on negative assumptions of what people can and will do. "The longer I survive," he told us, "the clearer I am about what I need and want to do. I will compromise to preserve my job and my organization. But I cannot go along with some of what I'm asked to do."

The reference in Paul's statement to the political and social changes of 1989 and 1990 does not escape us. There has been a certain irony associated with writing about fear in the American workplace when we know that each day, in countries far less democratic than ours, people take enormous risks to speak out. In China, Eastern Europe, South Africa, and Central and South America, people engage in acts of extraordinary personal and political courage, sometimes placing their lives at stake for the privileges we take for granted—one of which is self-expression.

Their actions make us feel a little foolish, considering that in "the land of the free and the home of the brave" so many do not feel free to speak up about their concerns at work. From the stories we have heard, we are convinced that each day too many of us—at all levels, in all types of jobs and roles—perpetuate dependent, bureaucratic, and autocratic work environments. While these actions are largely unconscious, the impact is unacceptable: self-generated and self-imposed patterns of fear and mistrust that restrict collective creativity, energy, and innovation. But we also see great possibilities and place our faith in an irrepressible national heritage that values independent thinking, risk taking, and the exploration of unknown territory.

A CHANGING VIEW OF PEOPLE

Most of us, like Paul, work in slightly schizophrenic organizations: traditional hierarchies that contain the seeds of new thinking and new energy. We may still feel the cycle of mistrust, with its low opinion of people, its distances and threats. But in the foreground there is an emerging faith and optimism. The low opinion of employees that has been inherited from the hierarchy is beginning to dissipate. The focus is increasingly on what *we* can do, *our* positive motives and intentions, *our* willingness to help. "Them" and "us" is no longer a satisfactory or inevitable mindset. We are discovering that we all want the same positive experiences at work; we all want to be proud of what we do and the organizations we work for. We want to use our skills constructively, contributing to a quality product or service valued by others. We want to be listened to, respected, appreciated, and trusted. And increasingly, there are managers who want to facilitate the transformation to the quality organization in which these discoveries are a way of life.

Therefore, while the road is long, there is already cause for rejoicing. Leaders like Paul are excited about the future and what it will mean for organizations. These leaders are people who possess a vision, have courage, and operate from the belief that successful organizations develop people, not intimidate them. The bright future they see depends on their ability to meet the challenges and hard times head-on, working as partners with their bosses, peers, and employees. They understand this basic criterion for success with their brains and their hearts and know that the results are more than long-term financial gains. They feel the pride that flows from empowering good people to do good work. They celebrate the confidence and insight which result from taking risks and trying new approaches. They are willing to work with things the way they are and, in doing so, they derive their satisfaction from making a great difference in a world ready for positive change.

REFERENCES

■

Argyris, C. "Skilled Incompetence." *The Harvard Business Review,* Sept.–Oct. 1986, pp. 74–79.

Argyris, C., Putnam, R., and Smith, D. M. *Action Science: Concepts, Methods, and Skills for Research and Intervention.* San Francisco: Jossey-Bass, 1985.

Bartolomé, F., and Laurent, A. "The Manager: Master and Servant of Power." *The Harvard Business Review,* Nov.–Dec. 1986, pp. 71–81.

Block, P. *The Empowered Manager: Positive Political Skills at Work.* San Francisco: Jossey-Bass, 1987.

Deming, W. E. *Out of the Crisis.* Cambridge, Mass.: MIT Press, 1986.

Fisher, R., and Brown, S. *Getting Together.* Boston: Houghton Mifflin, 1988.

Gibb, J. R. "Defensive Communication." *The Journal of Communication,* 1961, *11* (3), 141–148.

Gibb, J. R. "Fear and Facade: Defensive Management." In R. E. Farson (ed.), *Science and Human Affairs.* Palo Alto, Calif.: Science and Behavior Books, 1965.

Gibb, J. R. *Trust.* Los Angeles: Guild of Tutors Press, 1978.

Gitlow, H. S., and Gitlow, S. J. *The Deming Guide to Quality and Competitive Position.* Englewood Cliffs, N.J.: Prentice-Hall, 1987.

Hall, G. E. "The Concerns-Based Approach to Facilitating Change." *Educational Horizons,* 1979, *57* (4), 202–208.

Harvey, J. B. *The Abilene Paradox.* Lexington, Mass.: Lexington Books, 1988.

Kouzes, J. M., and Posner, B. Z. *The Leadership Challenge: How to Get Extraordinary Things Done in Organizations.* San Francisco: Jossey-Bass, 1987.

Lowe, T., and McBean, G. "Honesty Without Fear." *Quality Progress,* Nov. 1989, pp. 30–34.

McGregor, D. *The Professional Manager.* New York: McGraw-Hill, 1967.

Moore, M., and Gergen, P. "Risk Taking and Organization Change." *Training and Development Journal,* 1985, *39* (6), 72–76.

Moore, M., and Gergen, P. "Turning the Pain of Change into Creativity and Structure for the New Order." In R. H. Kilman, T. J. Covin, and Associates, *Corporate Transformation: Revitalizing Organizations for a Competitive World*. San Francisco: Jossey-Bass, 1988.

Rachman, S. J. *Fear and Courage*. San Francisco: W. H. Freeman, 1978.

Scherkenbach, W. W. *The Deming Route to Quality and Productivity: Roadmaps and Roadblocks*. Rockville, Md.: Mercury Press, 1986.

Shepard, H. "Rules of Thumb for Change Agents." *The OD Practitioner,* 1975, 7 (3).

Stowell, S. J., and Starcevich, M. M. *The Coach: Creating Partnerships for a Competitive Edge*. Salt Lake City, Utah: Center for Management and Organization Effectiveness, 1987.

Stringer, D. M., Pepitone-Arreola Rockwell, F., and Pearl, T. "Impacts on Employees of Abuse by Supervisors in the Workplace." Unpublished paper, 1989.

Tannenbaum, R., and Schmidt, W. "How to Choose a Leadership Pattern." *Harvard Business Review,* 1957, *36,* 95–100.

Weisbord, M. R. *Productive Workplaces: Organizing and Managing for Dignity, Meaning, and Community*. San Francisco: Jossey-Bass, 1987.

Zand, D. E. "Trust and Administrative Problem Solving." *Administrative Sciences Quarterly,* 1972, *17,* 229–239.

INDEX